D0734781

CURRY

To my parents

THE STORY OF THE
NATION'S FAVOURITE DISH

SHRABANI BASU

SUTTON PUBLISHING

First published in 1999 by HarperCollins India as
Curry in the Crown.

Revised and updated version published in 2003 by
Sutton Publishing Limited · Phoenix Mill
Thrupp · Stroud · Gloucestershire · GL5 2BU

British Library Cataloguing in Publication Data
A catalogue record for this book is available from the British
Library.

ISBN 0-7509-3374-7

Disclaimer: The various recipes presented within
this book have been taken from travellers' notes
and housewives' records and are for purposes of
illustration. Neither the author nor the publisher
can vouch for their authenticity or safety, and
accept no responsibility for any results
consequent upon their use.

Typeset in 11.5/15pt Melior.
Typesetting and origination by
Sutton Publishing Limited.
Printed and bound in England by
J.H. Haynes & Co. Ltd, Sparkford.

Contents

Acknowledgements

So many people have been part of this book that it is almost impossible to thank everybody individually. I would like to begin by thanking all those in the curry industry in Britain who gave me their valuable time and helped with the project.

In particular, I would like to thank Amin Ali, Sherin Alexander, Vineet Bhatia, Samar Hamid, Peter Grove, Atul Kochhar, Namita and Camelia Panjabi, Alfred Prasad, Rajesh Suri, Adi Modi and Iqbal Wahhab for sharing with me their wonderful insights into the restaurant business.

My thanks also to G.K. Noon, Kirit and Meena Pathak and Perween Warsi for sharing their life stories in such depth.

I would like to thank Jaqueline Mitchell, commissioning editor at Sutton Publishing, for her enthusiasm for the book. Thanks are also due to my editors, Matthew Brown and Jane Entrican, for their patience and support.

My thanks to Aveek Sarkar, editor of *Ananda Bazar Patrika*, for his constant encouragement. I would also like to thank my sisters Nupur and Moushumi for their moral support, and my brother-in-law Sanjeev for his constant supply of ideas and for discovering the nineteenth-century handwritten curry recipes at the Wellcome Institute Library.

And finally, thanks to my husband Dipankar for cooking the curries and my daughters Sanchita and Tanaya for keeping the noise levels down. Small mercies!

Shrabani Basu
Spetember 2003

Introduction

It was at the Spice of India in Wembley Park that I had my first curry. I remember running through the menu with some bewilderment, eating poppadoms with pickle (something I'd never done in India), and then finding to my surprise that the entire staff in the restaurant were from Bangladesh. My friendly Bengali-speaking waiter recommended that I try the lamb madras (another unfamiliar dish) and then popped his next question: 'Mild, medium or hot?' As I hesitantly said 'medium', he gave me a reassuring smile. 'I make it proper for you', he said, probably guessing that I was a curry novice. 'Not like theirs.' This last comment was illustrated with a conspiratorial nod at the other tables, which were full of English families obviously enjoying their plate-loads of naan, kebabs and fiery red curries. That was 1987 and I was soon to discover that the 'curry' – as Indian food was referred to in Britain – was a hot favourite among the British. And of course, that it was cooked differently for them.

I soon found that there were Indian restaurants on nearly every high street in Britain and that ready-made Indian meals could be bought at all the supermarkets. 'Going out for a curry' was a regular Friday night treat and as English as watching football and *Eastenders*.

The use of the word 'curry' to describe Indian food was slightly baffling. It is not a term used by Indians in India. There is the North Indian yoghurt-based preparation called 'Karhi' and there is the fragrant herb called 'curry leaf' – a favourite in South Indian cuisine – but there is nothing in India quite as universal as the British curry. The word itself was a British invention, and its origins probably lay a few hundred years back, in the days of the British Empire.

A commonly-held theory, first set out in *Hobson Jobson*, a dictionary of Anglo-Indian phrases (first published in 1886) is that the word evolved from the Tamil *kari*, meaning a sauce or a relish that accompanied rice. This is how *Hobson Jobson* described it: 'The proper office of *curry* in native diet. It consists of meat, fish, fruit or vegetables, cooked with a quantity of bruised spices and turmeric and a little of this gives a flavour to a large mess of rice.'

Whatever its historical origins, curry has now come to mean any number of hot, spicy and gravy-based dishes from the Indian subcontinent. For good or bad, curry is what describes Indian food today in the West. There is also a campaign to have the word 'curryholic' included in the Oxford dictionary.

A 1997 Gallup poll in Britain revealed that curry was beyond doubt the nation's favourite food, with over a quarter of Britons eating it at least once a week. Gallup concluded that Britain was becoming a nation of 'curryholics'. If indeed there was a time when the sun never set on the British Empire, the roles were reversed now. From John o'Groats to Land's End, an island nation of sixty million had truly been conquered by the curry. The United Kingdom's eating habits had changed for ever.

So much so that the former foreign secretary, Robin Cook, kicked off his election campaign in 2001 with his famous 'chicken tikka' speech, using the chicken tikka as a symbol of Britain's multiculturalism. The nation, he said, had not only made it its own but had modified it and created a new cuisine, all of which went to show that Britain had moved on from its colonial past and Anglo-Saxon image to being a flourishing multi-ethnic society. And the humble chicken tikka – according to Cook – was its colourful symbol.

Although Cook's speech was met with uncomfortable rumbles from the establishment, the undeniable point was that Britain's favourite food had received its final endorsement. There was no getting away from the fact that curry had become a way of life for the British.

Today, there are nearly 8,500 Indian restaurants in Britain – up from 3,500 in 1982 – visited by two million people each week. Each year £2 billion is spent in Indian restaurants – about £70 per second. Indian restaurants are the fastest growing in the restaurant business and even survived the mid-nineties recession. Some curry watchers hold that there are now more Indian restaurants in Britain than in New Delhi and Bombay put together and that London may soon become the curry capital of the world. Two Indian restaurants in London have now won Michelin stars and Indian food is becoming trendy, fashionable and upmarket.

As early as 1994, a survey by Mintel, the marketing company, showed that there was nothing the British liked better than to settle down with a dish of hot Indian curry. And they did not just depend on restaurants to serve them either. The curry had so wooed the English palate that the British were spending most of their grocery bills on buying Indian spices, curry pastes and chilled meals, according to the survey.

The same year, *Marketing* magazine's annual survey of the biggest brands in Britain named Patak's, the popular manufacturers of Indian pickles and pastes, as the fastest growing brand, with 92 per cent growth in retail sales in 1993. In second place with 71 per cent was Always sanitary towels manufactured by Procter and Gamble and third was Eternity, Calvin Klein's popular fragrance for men with 45 per cent growth. 'It came as something of a shock to find our fastest growing brand is owned not by a multi-national with an advertising budget to match but by a family-owned foods company', the magazine wrote. It was a veritable coup for proprietors Kirit and Meena Pathak who had bowled over British industry with a whiff of spice.

The supermarkets also saw a huge rise in Indian food in both the chilled and frozen sections. Marks & Spencer, one of Britain's leading department stores and where the Food Hall has always been popular, serves forty-five types of Indian dish and says every new dish is quickly snapped up by customers. Britons eat ten packs of Marks & Spencer's curry every minute of the day – enough portions in a year to give one to each of the nine million people who live in Bombay. Ironically, when Marks & Spencer went through a slump in sales in the late 1990s and was forced to close its store in Paris, the French were upset not because they would miss the lingerie, but because they would no longer be able to buy their favourite chicken tikka sandwiches for lunch.

The chain sells as many as eighteen tonnes of chicken tikka masala each week, confirming it as Britain's favourite Indian meal. Ironically, the chicken tikka masala (or CTM as it is known in the trade) is not a dish that you find in India. It is a peculiarly British curry invented in Britain for and by the British (probably Bangladeshi) cook. Ironically, this particular curry – for such is its fame – is now being served in some top restaurants in India as a novelty dish. It is, of course, frowned upon by authentic Indian chefs and restaurateurs in Britain and many upmarket restaurants would not dream of serving it to their clients now. However, it is this dish that has consistently been voted the favourite curry and perhaps the dish that caused a quiet culinary revolution. Robin Cook's famous chicken tikka speech was not without cause.

Even Britain's most exclusive department store, Harrods, lays on the curry heavily. The famed Harrods Food Hall has a wide range of Indian meals in the deli counter. These include chicken korma, chicken jalfrezi, chicken malabari, reshmi kebab, lazeez kebab, niligiri gosht korma, lasooni jhinga, malai tikka, biriani, and various sauces, chutneys and pickles. Here again the most popular are the chicken tikka masala, tandoori chicken, sweet and sour aubergine, Bombay potatoes, biriani and daal.

Whether it is the elegant Fortnum & Mason in Piccadilly or the fashionable Harvey Nichol's in Knightsbridge, there is a place for curry. Both stores have a range of tandoori pastes and curry sauces on their well-stocked shelves. There is a Fortnum & Mason brand of vindaloo and korma in both medium and hot flavours, while Harvey Nichol's has its own brand of curry sauces. Chutneys, poppadoms and elegant small tins of basmati rice form part of their exotic Indian selection.

Gone are the days of the fifties and sixties when English landladies would stop their Indian tenants from cooking curries because it made the house smell. Today the British are cooking it for themselves, helped by an elaborate range of curry pastes available in the supermarkets and popularised by celebrity chefs like Jamie Oliver who liberally spice up their food with bunches of coriander and Indian spices.

Given the curry mania, it was hardly surprising, therefore, that England's (unofficial) song for the 1998 Football World Cup was called 'Vindaloo'. Bemused Parisians watched as English fans, their faces painted with the flag of St George with its red cross on white, lustily sang about curry power. The song went as follows:

> Where on earth are you from? We're from
>   Eng-er-land
> Me and me mum and me dad and me gran
> We're off to Waterloo
> Me and me mum and me dad and me gran
> And a bucket of vindaloo.

If the French were wondering why the English were singing a song about Indian curry, Robin Cook would no doubt have explained it to them. For if the sea of English painted faces had one thing in common, apart from their devotion to football, it was their fanatical love of curry. 'Vindaloo', the pop song, shot to number one in the charts. And Marks & Spencer, in keeping with the curry spirit, immediately laid out a vindaloo ready-meal range in full style. It was the football season after all.

That football and curry went together could not have been more obvious. England failed to get into the finals, but what of it? A group of ten Scottish fans in Bordeaux became so homesick for their curry, they ordered a £1,400 Indian takeaway from a restaurant in Bournemouth, south-east England.

The food was specially flown out to Bordeaux in time for a Scotland–Norway match. For its well-publicised pains, the Eye of the Tiger restaurant, which regularly flies out orders of Indian meals around the world, charged a hefty £600 for the food and £800 for the delivery by chartered plane.

Curry has even become a leveller of sorts. What used to be a meal for the discerning middle classes, for those who knew about India and world food, has now become a household name transcending all classes. Even the toughest tattooed football fan with a couple of pints of lager in him, returning home from cheering his team at Wembley or Old Trafford, knows his rogan josh from his lamb madras and will not hesitate to point it out if the local Karahi King serves him otherwise.

Even the British Tourist Authority capitalised on currymania in the late 1990s. Tourist guides boldly stated that curry was the number one British dish, and if you thought it was, well, fish and chips, you had a 'misplaced sense of island tradition'. In trying to erase some of the stereotypical images of Britain as a country of castles, foggy skies and divorcing royalty, the Tourist Authority chose the hot curry to promote cool Britannia. Exciting and contemporary Britain is 'turning into a nation of curryholics', said the guide. 'Actress and curry guru Madhur Jaffrey has become the Mrs Beeton of the 1990s.'

The British government, too, recognised the importance of curry in the British diet. Towards the end of 1999, when there were fears that the Millennium Bug would hit supplies of essential items as Britons entered the Year 2000, the head of the government's Millennium Bug Task Force Action 2000 asked citizens to stock up with at least two weeks' supplies before the turn of the century. On Gwyneth Flower's official list of essential items were: 'tins, dried food and grain, cans of soup, *half a dozen curries* [italics mine], tuna and packets of biscuit and longlife milk'. The message was clear: if things were going to be disrupted, don't get caught out without your curry.

The times, it seems, have truly changed for the old cod or haddock. The once popular local chippie is slowly becoming a thing of the past. The tandoori chicken has arrived. How often over the last decade have I seen fish and chip shops either shut down or reinvent themselves to serve kebabs and tikkas as well.

The daily newspapers often carry many stories about British curryholics who would do anything for their curry. On one occasion, a road accident victim in the north of England famously asked bemused onlookers for a curry before he asked for an ambulance. Magistrates in York digested the following first words of Derek Bond upon regaining consciousness after being hit by a speeding car: 'Phone my wife and tell her to keep my curry warm.' He had been on his way home from work and Mrs Bond evidently had a hot curry waiting for him. Mr Bond did not get his curry that night, but there was no deterring him. 'My wife heated up the curry in the morning and I had it for breakfast. I was determined not to miss out on my Saturday night treat', he said later.

Radio DJ Lisa l'Anson was not far behind, having once paid £1,525 to have her curry flown to Miami after discovering that Indian food was not available there. In fact, such is the addiction to curry that Mustapha Aolad of the Eye of the Tiger restaurant runs a flying curry service (he is a qualified pilot from Bangladesh) to places as far off as Sydney, New York and Tokyo. He is planning a restaurant in the sky in a Boeing 707, so that diners looking for the ultimate curry experience can fly over London by night, looking down at Big Ben while tucking into their chicken madras and prawn vindaloo. And the national carrier, British Airways, has begun providing curry meals on most of its long-haul flights, not just those flying to the Indian subcontinent. Passengers flying to New York, Johannesburg or Sydney can now tuck into the all-time favourite chicken tikka masala, basmati pilau and vegetarian dishes.

As curry becomes a way of life in Britain, it isn't just about eating curry either. Curry hit the air waves as Talk Radio created an on-air curry poem. Listeners across the country called the station's breakfast show with their poetry lines. Presenter Paul Ross said the lines were jammed and at the end of the show they had a great poem. It went something like this: 'You're hot, you're there. You want me to eat you/Your pungent beauty with a radiant hue . . .' Pretty hot stuff.

Apart from humans, it seems British fish are also developing a taste for the stuff! Fisherman Phil Wilding won an angling competition by flavouring his maggots with curry powder. Wilding claimed the fish simply could not resist the gorgeous smell wafting from his bait.

Curry is flavouring politics in Britain too: the Indo-British Parliamentary Group is called the Curry Club. Comprising some sixty British MPs with an interest in India, it is jointly headed by a member of the ruling party in Britain and the Indian High Commissioner, and meets over working curry lunches. Usually held at the Indian High Commission or the High Commissioner's residence, the sit-down lunch is always a curry. Often an Indian dignitary who is passing through is invited. In the past, former Indian Prime Ministers P.V. Narasimha Rao and V.P. Singh have attended Curry Club dos, and issues ranging from Kashmir to foreign investments have been discussed over delectable kebabs and tikkas.

If the way to an Englishman's heart is through a curry, then British politicians have surely been wooed with a fair share of curry diplomacy. But why stop at MPs? Signs are that curry has its fans at the highest level of the British political establishment.

On the opening day of the Labour Party annual conference in September 1998, Prime Minister Tony Blair and his wife Cherie decided on an Indian takeaway. While Tony calmed the nerves of the party faithful worried about the state of the economy, Cherie popped over to the local Sunam

Tandoori and ordered a meal of poppadoms, chicken tikka masala, lamb madras, some vegetables and daal for eighteen members of Tony's entourage. In true no-nonsense takeaway style, the bill was marked 'For Mr Blair' and came to only £185, which proved that when it comes to value for money, there is no beating a curry.

From posh Blairites to ordinary people, Britain's love of curry crosses the class divide. Even Britain's celebrity couple, David Beckham and wife Victoria (Posh) Spice, have said that their favourite TV dinner is a curry. When the Indian cricket team toured England in the summer of 2002, they were treated to a fabulous curry dinner at the Yorkshire house of former England cricketer Geoffrey Boycott, who proved that a Batley curry could match anything from Bombay. And when another former England cricketer, Ian Botham, decided to walk for charity from John o'Groats to Land's End, no prizes for guessing what he ordered to keep himself going. It was, of course, five hundred curries.

The British have not only been eating and cooking curries, they have been innovating with surprising enthusiasm. Traditional English lamb is being roasted with Indian spices instead of the usual mint. Pizzas come with chicken tikka toppings and even the sacrosanct Christmas turkey is now being marinated with Indian spices. Cardamom, cloves and cumin seeds are being used more and more in regular cooking, and under the influence of celebrity television chefs, coriander is used to flavour many dishes.

Popular Chinese chef Ken Hom once revealed that he always carried a packet of madras hot curry powder with him and that he used it to dash up all his meals and even his salads. Ken Hom may have been surprised to learn that curry powder itself is not an authentic Indian spice but created by the British in India as a convenient spice for taking back home to England or to be used without the effort of grinding fresh spices.

While some die-hard Indian cooks have problems with curry powder, close followers of the curry industry in Britain, such as writer and gourmet cook Pat Chapman, have no quarrel with it. Chapman, who started the Curry Club in Britain in 1982 (not to be confused with the MPs club of the same name) and who publishes a yearly *Good Curry Guide* (a list of Britain's top 1,000 restaurants), will tell you that authenticity doesn't really matter. It tastes good, people like it, and that's the way it should be. After all, food is about experimentation and innovation.

British innovation with Indian food extends to chicken tikka sandwiches and balti pies, and up north in Scotland, haggis pakoras. Even traditional English sauces have taken on new flavours: market research has shown that Britons prefer curry, madras and korma sauces to stroganoff and chasseur. And in the run-up to Christmas, curry recipes are as regular as the roasts and Christmas pies. A quick search on the web once revealed a Santa Claus website which had among other things: recipes for traditional, vegetarian and

Indian food. Even Mrs Claus, it seems, could not escape the call of the curry.

The Indian food business has produced a string of millionaires in Britain. Most of them began their careers churning out samosas and pickles in their kitchens and selling them in small shops and retail units. Now they employ anything from 500–600 workers each and have turnovers of millions. The big names in the food industry are Perween Warsi, head of S & A Foods, and Sir Gulam Khaderboy Noon, head of Noon Products, suppliers of chilled meals to supermarkets, and informally called the 'Curry King'. The Pathaks, who bought pickles and pastes to every household in Britain, are an institution in themselves.

If the Pathaks provided the spices, cookery experts like Madhur Jaffrey popularised curry by guiding millions of television viewers on how to serve up an exotic Indian meal without much fuss. Jaffrey's natural talent at step-by-step cooking made the six-part BBC television series *Flavours of India* one of the most popular programmes of the early nineties. The accompanying book sold thousands of copies. As Jaffrey became the official curry ambassador, recognised even by the British Tourist Authority, she launched her own brand of sauces in partnership with the leading basmati rice manufacturers, Tilda. The range of Tilda–Madhur Jaffrey pastes are a familiar sight on supermarket shelves. A portrait of Madhur Jaffrey even hangs at the National Portrait Gallery as part of a series on famous British chefs.

How did Indian food become this popular, and who has the honour of having changed the way Britons eat today? The answer, of course, lies in Britain's colonial history. At the end of the Raj, the British returned to England having developed a taste for spices. In the early fifties they longed for the food they had left behind. At the same time the first of the Bangladeshi immigrants arrived. They had been dock workers, or crew on board P&O ships, and learnt to cook a variety of dishes from fellow crew members, who were often from south India or France.

Later, looking for jobs in their newly adopted home, the Bangladeshis put their newly acquired culinary skills to good use in earning a living. Slowly the numbers of Indian restaurants began to grow. They were all Bangladeshi-owned, with cooks from the district of Sylhet churning out the curries. The restaurants were usually family-run with relatives and friends chipping in to help. The community spirit kept the restaurants going through lean days, busy weekends and late nights. The food was good, cheap and, most importantly, it was moulded for the British palate. Soon it had everybody hooked.

The only thing that gave them away – and to someone reasonably familiar with the Indian subcontinent – were the names of the restaurants. Inevitably the restaurants would be called the Golden Bengal Tandoori, the Sylhet Tandoori or Bengal Balti. This was delightfully ironic because the traditional cuisine of Bengal is neither tandoori nor balti. (Bengalis eat fish and rice cooked in a very different style and you won't find a tandoori masala in a traditional Bengali kitchen.)

Shrewdly, the Bangladeshi restaurants stuck to north Indian dishes like tandoori chicken and tikkas which are mild and popular. Chilli was usually added by personal request ('Would madam like it hot, medium or mild?') and the food was prepared for the British palate. The food usually all tasted the same because it was prepared from the same curry base. It was not sophisticated or authentic Indian, but it was what the British were pining for, and what they were served. The Indian restaurant earned a new label: cheap and cheerful.

There is little doubt that it is the hard work put in by the entrepreneurial Bangladeshis over the past four decades that has laid the foundation of the curry revolution. Nearly 80 per cent of Indian restaurants in Britain are owned by Bangladeshis, and mainly from one particular area – Sylhet.

Today there isn't a corner of Britain, from the tiniest village in the heart of Wales to the remotest of Scottish highlands to industrial towns in the Midlands, that doesn't have a curry restaurant. It is as much a part of the landscape as the village parish church, the craft shop, the pub and the local post office. The polite owner will always be from Bangladesh and his restaurant will almost certainly be called the Jewel in the Crown, or the Gurkha Tandoori, or the Taj Mahal or Maharajah. The decor will be predictable, the menu pretty uniform, but the food and service will always be good value for money.

Bangladeshi-owned restaurants have an annual turnover of £2 billion, paying over £250 million in value added tax and serving two million covers a week. More than 50,000 people are employed by them, more than the total British workforce in steels and mines.

With economic success has come the beginnings of organisational activity. Bangladeshi restaurateurs have launched the Guild of Bangladeshi Restaurateurs in London which now wants to serve Bangladeshi food and invest in training. But the Dine Bangladeshi campaign also wants Indian restaurants to be known as Bangladeshi restaurants, an idea which has not found many takers.

The organisational strength of Bangladeshis in the restaurant business became evident in March 1998 when Iqbal Wahhab, the editor of *Tandoori Magazine*, a popular trade magazine, caused a stir by describing Indian waiters as 'miserable gits' who made dining out feel like 'going to a funeral'.

Following widespread coverage of the comment in the mainstream media, Iqbal Wahhab, himself a Bangladeshi, was sacked. The magazine published grovelling apologies spread over several pages as Wahhab and his proprietors faced the combined wrath of some 40,000 Bangladeshi waiters who threatened to stop serving and stocking Cobra Indian beer which sponsors the magazine. Curry war was big news. After all, no less than a nation's cuisine was at stake.

Eventually Wahhab opened his own upmarket restaurant, the Cinnamon Club, in the Old

Westminster Library, abandoned the CTM and poppadoms so favoured by his fellow Bangladeshi restaurateurs, and prayed for a Michelin star. Lord Andrew Lloyd Webber chose to have the launch party for his latest musical, *Bombay Dreams*, at the Cinnamon Club and so the story had a happy ending. The Cinnamon Club was back in the news in March 2003 when it was revealed that fire brigade union leader, Andy Gilchrist, had spent £817.31 on a meal at the restaurant with four other colleagues, consuming vintage wines at £85.00 a bottle. Wahhab's restaurant was clearly a far cry from high-street curry houses.

Predictably, the tabloids next day responded by saying it was far too much to spend at an Indian restaurant, and listed all the things that Gilchrist and his colleagues could have bought in an ordinary curry house for the same amount. Curry was always news.

The revolution started by the slap-up curry and rice has truly swept the nation. Every kitchen in Britain has been invaded and a people's cuisine transformed. The Bangladeshi curry crusaders showed the way, the spice traders picked up the business, the huge influx of immigrants in the 1970s provided the market and workforce and curry eventually took its place on supermarket shelves: chilled or frozen, ready to be carted home, put in the microwave and washed down with a pint of lager.

Today, nearly every department store from Selfridges to John Lewis and Woolworths stocks

Indian cooking vessels, stainless steel and cast-iron karahis, steel plates and bowls, usually accompanied by Indian recipe books and spice jars.

The cuisine itself kept evolving as restaurateurs introduced new flavours. Hard on the heels of the tandoori craze came the balti rage in the mid-eighties and early nineties. Starting in the Midlands, the cuisine is said to showcase the flavours of Baltistan, an area in northern Pakistan. But some claimed that the name came from the meals that were served up in an Indian restaurant in Birmingham quite literally from a *balti* (bucket). The cuisine is somewhat different from tandoori in that it is more gravy-based and is eaten with naan bread. Inevitably, Birmingham's balti restaurants went national and a spate of them popped up all over the place. Chilled meals, pastes and the supermarkets followed suit and balti briefly became a cult cuisine.

From the mid-nineties the balti craze faded, although it is still popular in the Midlands. Karahi dishes now came into vogue. Restaurants with names like Lahore Karahi, Bengal Karahi, and Karahi King suddenly appeared on high streets. Supermarkets followed predictably with a new karahi range. The karahi was a bigger success story than the balti because it was closer to authentic Indian cooking.

And the latest in the market is Indian regional cuisine. Enter the cuisine of Goa, the Malabar Coast, Kerala and Andhra Pradesh. As Indian restaurants try to get away from the flock wallpaper, laminated menus and tandoori dishes, they are becoming more upmarket, more daring and more innovative. They have begun to serve regional and specialist cuisine prepared by chefs imported from India (as opposed to Bangladeshi chefs), bringing an entirely new variety of cuisine to British consumers. Fusion cuisine has entered the market and Indian chefs are experimenting and creating new dishes. Two chefs, Vineet Bhatia (of Zaika) and Atul Kochhar (formerly of Tamarind), have recently won Michelin stars and are taking Indian cuisine in Britain into the twenty-first century.

With Indian food emerging as a profitable business, nearly all the players in the field have ambitious expansion plans. Many have begun to export to other European countries. Indian food is already making its presence felt in Paris, Brussels and Amsterdam, the three cities with the largest number of Indian restaurants on the Continent. Most companies also export to the USA, Canada and the Gulf countries.

Back in Britain, Indian food has overtaken the Chinese food industry, previously the most popular international cuisine. As British cooks throw away the chip pan and pick up the karahi, Indian food has also been recognised as being more healthy. It is now commonly known that eating curry can give you a feel-good factor and some ingredients in a curry – turmeric, ginger and garlic, for instance – have curative properties.

Indian cuisine is seen to be healthier than junk food such as burgers, French fries and fried chicken and the number of takers is increasing every day.

Britain now has a National Curry Day and annual competitions to find the Curry Chef of the Year. In fact it hasn't been Indian or Bangladeshi chefs alone who have carried off these awards. In 1997 the award went to Simon Morris, head chef of Grafton Manor, a country-house hotel in the Midlands, and in 1998 the International Indian chef award went to 33-year-old Niall Gordon from Surrey who beat Indian chefs to walk off with the prize cheque.

The British today have become more discerning about their rogan josh than their roast beef. As Andy Gilchrist discovered, a nation of curry watchers examined his orders at the Cinnamon Club (replicated by several broadsheets) and engaged in a debate on high-street curry houses versus upmarket Indian restaurants. Only a curry could spark such passions.

1

On the Spice Trail

A scientist in Cambridge once recalled that when he returned to England after spending several years abroad, his colleague wanted to take him out to lunch. What kind of lunch would he like, the colleague asked. Something typically English, he replied with expatriate nostalgia. They ended up in an Indian restaurant for a curry.

In retrospect, there's nothing surprising about a curry being described as a typically English meal any more. Spicy eastern foods have become an enduring part of English cuisine, its roots going back to the days of the Raj and conjuring up memories of the Empire, tea, sprawling bungalows and verandahs, nimboo-panis, servants in livery, chota haziris, and slow-moving ceiling fans. They are as much part of the English menu as words like jodhpur, guru, pyjama, polo, gymkhana and bungalow are part of the English language. What was surprising about the two hundred years of colonial rule was that while all things English — railways, cricket, parliamentary democracy, education, the legal system — remained with India, the only significant thing that travelled back from India to England was the curry.

The story of the curry begins hundreds of years back in the cold dreary days of winter when an island nation needed spices to cure and preserve food over the long winter months. Ironically, it was the quest for spices that took the English to India, first as traders and then as rulers, leading to the chain of historical events that would see the two countries linked together for the next two centuries and beyond.

Spices, with their tingle and exoticism, brought a touch of colour and glamour to life in northern Europe which in the medieval period was lacking in both. Spices helped preservation, disguised the bland from the rancid and brought a taste of oriental glamour into the bleak English winter. It has been suggested that the major annual festivals – Christmas, Lent and Easter – all occurred in winter at the start, middle and end simply to liven up the cheerless winter months.

Spices were important to the Romans who established trading links to the Middle East and beyond. They exchanged their gold for spices and Venice and Genoa became prosperous using their maritime trade to establish connections with the ports on the Mediterranean. From the thirteenth to the fifteenth centuries, Venice monopolised the spice trade with the Middle East.

In Britain, the Norman conquest had introduced a new range of culinary spices. But these were all luxury items beyond the reach of the common man. Only the aristocracy could enjoy such exotic spices as cloves, cinnamon, cardamom, nutmeg, pepper, ginger, garlic and turmeric. These were used for cooking in the royal kitchens. So valuable were spices that they could be used in lieu of money. Pepper, the king of spices, virtually became a currency in its own right. Hence the origin of the term 'peppercorn rent'. Today it means a minimal sum of money, but in medieval times it meant 'at the market price paid in pepper'. A pound of pepper in twelfth-century London could buy you several sheep and it was used to pay taxes and debts.

Pepper, highly in demand, was reaching England through an elaborate network of Afghan, Persian, Arab, Venetian and northern European middlemen via the overland routes from India. Venice had the ultimate monopoly over these spices and the merchants demanded exorbitant prices.

It was to break this monopoly that Portugal and Spain started looking eastward for routes to the Spice Islands around the Cape of Good Hope. Holland, France and England were also keen to break the Italian monopoly and get their own foothold in the lucrative spice trade.

An era of high sea adventures was to be launched. By the fifteenth century European nations were jostling to locate the spices at source. With Venice firmly in control of the Mediterranean seas, the nations started exploring the oceans. Monarchs were enthusiastic about the crusaders and financed small fleets of adventurous mariners. It was the Spanish king who financed Christopher Columbus when he wanted to discover the fabulous wealth of India and China, thinking it lay just a few thousand miles away across the Atlantic. Columbus found the wrong continent, but it was the beginning of an era of maritime adventures started by the search for spices.

Five hundred years ago, towards the end of the fifteenth century, the Portuguese navigator Vasco da Gama arrived at the port of Kappad near Kozhikode (Calicut) after completing the first voyage from Europe to Asia around the Cape of Good Hope. It was a Gujarati from Kenya, Ibn Majid, who guided the Portuguese navigator from the ports of Malinithi in Kenya to Kappad. Vasco da Gama's purpose was to trade in spices and eliminate the middlemen: the Arabs who had monopolised the spice trade with Malabar and Malacca. There was also the natural Portuguese and Spanish Christian hostility to the Arabs or the Moors, who were among the earliest traders in India and with whom there had been previous conflict in Spain where the Moors had ruled for many centuries.

It was the crusades and the re-conquest of Granada by Queen Isabella of Spain which led to a new era of Spanish expansion overseas. Given Spain's new expansionist mood, King Manuel I of Portugal gave his full backing to da Gama when he set sail for India on the *Sao Gabriel*. On 27 May 1498, da Gama approached the port of Kozhikode. It was a buzzing port from where merchants carried spices and the famed calico to Egypt, Turkey and Europe. The coast was dotted with mansions built by the merchants. The ship avoided the town and dropped anchor near a cluster of huts. Taking a small boat, the Portuguese rode over the waters to where the village was clearly visible with the fishing boats and nets spread on the beach. This was Kappad, twenty kilometres south of Calicut. On disembarking, Vasco da Gama knelt and kissed the earth, holding up a crucifix. The arrival was a landmark step in Indian history. Even today there is a memorial on Kappad beach dedicated to da Gama's arrival. The 3-metre-long obelisk inscribed with da Gama's name marks his first steps on Indian soil.

After Vasco da Gama, another Portuguese explorer called Pedro Alvares Cabral was despatched to India and established a Portuguese trading post at Calicut. Those stationed in Calicut by Cabral were massacred and da Gama – who was called Admiral of India – was sent to avenge the act. He forced the rajah to make peace and, bearing a rich cargo of spices, left India in 1503 and sailed back to Portugal.

So lucrative was the trade in spices that the Portuguese took firm control of their exports. Each shipload consisted of fourteen items including fifteen hundred tonnes of round pepper, twenty-eight tonnes of ginger, nine tonnes of cinnamon and seven tonnes of cloves. Profits from their sales in Europe were enormous. It is estimated that the spices carried back by da Gama on his very first voyage itself paid for the cost of the entire operation six times over.

In 1513 the Portuguese re-established a trading post at Calicut, then a prosperous cotton weaving centre. Vasco da Gama made his third trip to India in 1524 and died in Cochin only three months after he arrived.

As the Europeans embarked on hazardous journeys across the seas in search of spices, it inevitably led to wars between the main rivals for the control of the spice-bearing coast. By the late fifteenth century, the Portuguese, Dutch, French and eventually the British all tried to set up coastal trading posts. The Portuguese, by far the leaders in the field, set up coastal trading posts and fortresses rather than settlement colonies. But by the late sixteenth century the tide had turned and their monopoly was seriously challenged by the English and the Dutch.

The English were latecomers to the spice race but were not to be outdone. Under Henry VIII, they had started to build a powerful navy with ocean-going ships. Under Queen Elizabeth I these started plundering Spanish vessels. Explorations had not yet begun. In 1577 explorer Francis Drake made the world's second circumnavigation. In 1588 Drake destroyed the famous Spanish Armada, making history and opening the seas for further English adventures.

The English at first wanted to control the Spice Islands which they called the East Indies. This brought them directly into conflict with the Dutch and the Portuguese. The first English ship was sent to the Spice Islands in 1591 but it was a disaster.

Insufficiently armed and ill-prepared, it was easily defeated by the Portuguese. The Dutch were quick to learn from the English defeat. They set up the Dutch East India Company, properly financed and with sufficient military strength to make expeditions. In 1595 they sent their first ship to the Spice Islands and routed the Portuguese. The Dutch were not disappointed: their first cargo of cloves made them a 2,500 per cent profit.

The Dutch victory led to some quick rethinking in the English camp. In 1599 a group of London merchants formed the East India Company, to get a toe-hold in the spice trade and primarily to bring down the price of pepper. In 1600 Queen Elizabeth I granted it the Royal Charter. It was one of her last acts in power and she was not to know at that stage that she was laying the foundations of empire.

The euphoria was high. Flushed with memories of the victory over the Spanish Armada eleven years previously, the East India Company set sail a fleet of ships to get a hold of the spices. The ships, charmingly called *Clove* and *Peppercorn*, were not fated to meet with success at sea. The Dutch were too well prepared for them and the English were forced to retreat.

They now began to look at their second destination and the original source of pepper: India. It was in 1608 that the first English ship carrying a minor company representative, Captain William Hawkins, landed in Surat in India. His mission was to try and secure a small trading base in India. After being kept waiting for three months, and despite a courteous reception by Emperor Jahangir, Hawkins found he could not obtain permission for a trading base. The Portuguese had worked behind the scene – having been established there from 1498 – and managed to influence Jahangir. Hawkins felt he had been treated shabbily, not just because of the Portuguese hold on Jahangir but because his mission was not impressive enough with gifts unworthy of the Mughal Emperor. He returned to England with a message for King James: to send better gifts for the Emperor and a more powerful fleet to take on the Portuguese.

In 1612 a second fleet was despatched, far better equipped, and by now focused entirely on the Indian subcontinent. It easily defeated the Portuguese fleet off Surat. Sir Thomas Roe, a new ambassador, was also despatched. The efficiency of the British victory now impressed Jahangir and he readily had an audience with Sir Thomas Roe. The English obtained their permission to set up a base and in 1618 the first factory was started in Surat. It was the beginning of what would later become the Empire. At Surat the English merchants were served 'dumpoked' (*dumpukht*) fowl, stewed in butter and stuffed with spices, almonds and raisins. The recipes came straight from the Mughal Emperor Akbar's kitchen and the English merchants pronounced the pilaus and birianis 'delicious'. It was also the start of their eastern culinary adventure.

At this period, gentlemen in England had still not started to use forks and the food was scooped and eaten by hand very much as with their Indian counterparts.

Jahangir thought the Mughals would benefit from an alliance with a naval power and was pleased to play down the Portuguese who had been fanatic in their religious outlook. Sir Thomas Roe looked like a man with whom Jahangir could do business and the English were given their point of entry. Roe remained ambassador at his court from 1615–19. He was a sophisticated man and was favourably disposed to India. It is recorded that he had both an Indian and an English cook, but insisted on eating his meals at the table except when dining with easterners.

Jahangir regularly sent Sir Thomas the meat of the chase; once a 'mighty elk' (perhaps a nilgai or sambhar), which he described as 'reasonably rank meat', and once wild boar, with a polite request that the 'tusks be returned'. Roe noted that Mughal nobles kept luxurious tables: up to twenty dishes were served at a time, sometimes even fifty.

Roe's chaplain, Revd Edward Terry, who spent three years in India, presented his account to the Prince of Wales (later Charles I) on his return. It was published along with accounts of other travellers by Revd Samuel Purchas in *Purchas and his Pilgrims*. It recalled of the Indians that

they feed not freely on full dishes of mutton and beef as we, but much on rice boiled with pieces of flesh or dressed many other ways. They have not many roast or baked meats, but stew most of their flesh. Among many dishes of this kind, I will take notice of one they call *deu pario* [do-pyaza] made of venison cut in slices, to which they put onions and herbs, some roots with a little spice and butter: the most savoury meat I have ever tasted and do almost think it that very dish which Jacob made ready for his father, when he got the blessing.

That the English traveller had a taste for Indian cookery as early as the seventeenth century is obvious from these writings. Terry also reports that at a dinner given to Sir Thomas Roe by Asaf Khan (brother of Nur Jahan and father of Mumtaz Mahal) the ambassador 'had more dishes than ten, and I less by ten than our entertainer had, yet for my part I had fifty dishes'. He went on:

Now, of the provision itself, for our large dishes, they were filled with rice dressed. And this rice was presented to us, some of it white, in its own proper colour, some of it yellow, with saffron, and some of it was made green, and some of it was put in purple colour . . . and with rice thus ordered, several of our dishes were furnished, and very many more of them with flesh of several kinds, and with hens and other sorts of fowl cut in pieces, as before observed in their Indian cookery. To these we had many jellie and culices; Rice ground to flour and then boyled and after sweetened with sugar, candy and rosewater to be eaten cold. The flower or rice mingled with sweet almonds, made as small as they could, and with some of the most fleshy parts hens, stewed with it and after, the flesh beaten to pieces, that it could not be discerned all made sweet with rosewater and sugar candy, and scented with ambergreece which was another of our dishes and a most luscious one, which the Portuguls call 'Manger Real', food for a king.

The French doctor Francois Bernier, who was physician to both Dara Shikoh and Emperor Aurangzeb, recorded about Bengal that

Meat is salted at a cheap rate by the Dutch and English for the supply of their vessels, fish of every species, whether fresh or salt, is in same profusion. In a word Bengal abounds with every necessity of life . . . [all of which] has given rise to a proverb among the Portuguese, English and Dutch that the kingdom of Bengal has a hundred gates open for entrance but not one for departure.

The English traveller in medieval India adapted readily to the culinary delights on offer: pilaus, kebabs, dum pukht, birianis and other delectables. It is interesting to note that chilli had just been introduced into Indian cuisine at the time, brought in by the Portuguese, who had discovered it in the New World. Before the chilli was introduced, the hottest Indian spices commonly used were mustard seeds and black peppercorns. Chillies are now an essential part of Indian cooking. The clove, too, was introduced to India at the beginning of the nineteenth century by the East India Company.

Soon the English were well on their way as traders in India. Trading stations were founded in Kozhikode by the East India Company in 1664. In 1683 the British won the right to set up a spice depot in Tellichery, a place famous for its high-quality Malabar pepper known for its aroma and size.

In 1698 the French also set up trading stations in Kozhikode. In 1790, when the local rajas tried to expel the European merchants, the British seized Kozhikode. By 1792 they had annexed the city with much of the surrounding region.

The East provided medieval Europe with its luxury goods: spices, jewellery and textiles. In exchange, Europe sold woollen garments, the Dutch sold salted herrings and the Spanish and French exported salt. India bought copper and Persian carpets.

What began with the spice trade soon grew into trade in primary products. After 1850, trade in grain and wool also expanded. Europe imported wheat from North America, Australia, Argentina and India, paying for its products with products of industry.

As the Europeans settled in, the taste for Indian food continued to grow. The early Europeans enjoyed Indian food as it was enjoyed by the locals and the aristocracy. A BBC Radio 4 programme in August 1998 tried to recreate the meal Robert Clive would have had after the Battle of Plassey in 1757. Restaurateur Namita Panjabi, who recreated the dishes in the studio, said they would have eaten traditional nawabi Indian food like chicken dopiaza, *malai chingri* (prawns in coconut cream sauce) and biriani among other things.

The fusion foods or the Anglo-Indian cuisine of the Raj years would come much later. But 'curry' – or meat and vegetables in gravy – was already identified and enjoyed by the English. William Hawkins had recorded it as early as 1608 and his observations found their way into *Hobson Jobson*, the ultimate Anglo-Indian phrase book first published in 1886, and described in the Introduction.

In the eighteenth century the main meal was in the middle of the day, followed by a siesta, evening visits and light dinner. The English in India were already laying lavish tables and meals were being prepared and served by an army of servants and *khidmutgars*. In 1780 in Calcutta, Mrs Eliza Fay, a lawyer's wife and herself a dressmaker by trade, wrote in *Original Letters from India*, edited by E.M. Forster:

We dine at two o'clock in the very heat of the day . . . a soup, a roast fowl, curry and rice, a mutton pie, forequarter of lamb, a rice pudding, tarts, very good cheese, fresh churned butter and excellent Madeira.

Already the cuisine was changing from what Thomas Roe and Revd Terry had enjoyed, which was traditional Indian food. The arrival of the memsahib meant that some aspects of English cooking were introduced and incorporated into the main meal, exemplified by Mrs Fay's lunchtime spread.

But while the householder was eating a mix of both Indian and English, the single Englishman without his family, living in messes and hostels all over the land, depended on his Indian cook and was already addicted to his culinary turnovers. In a commentary on medical conditions in India by Norman Chievers, surgeon general, HM Indian Army, published by J. and A. Churchill in London in 1886, Chievers reports:

In India, every native man and woman is a 'good plain cook' and every bawarchee, however unskilled, sends daily to his master's table such a dinner as place in great danger of becoming a gourmand the ex-student who has for years grown more and more dyspeptic in battening upon the smoked and scorched flesh with which his lodging house drudge has provided him . . . Anyone who imagines that the Indian heat spoils our appetites is greatly mistaken, and any, who in England have been accustomed to dine of a plain joint and pudding, and to take little beyond an egg or rasher with their bread and butter at breakfast often fall into the great error of eating highly seasoned meats at each of their daily meals.

The poet Edward Lear had a breakfast while in India in 1874 of boiled prawns, prawn curry, cold mutton, bread and butter and plantain. And that was just the start of his day.

While the English were enjoying Indian food in India, thousands of miles away curries were being cooked in English kitchens as well. In fact, Queen Victoria herself was known to insist on a curry every day being prepared at her holiday retreat in Osborne House on the Isle of Wight, where she spent the most relaxed years of her life.

Fascinated by India, though she never went there, the Empress of India tried to learn as much about the country from her Indian servants, in particular her favourite secretary, Abdul Karim or Munshiji. On her Golden Jubilee in 1887 she was presented with two Indian servants, Sheikh Ghulam Mustafa and Sheikh Chidda. They were essentially table hands and would stand behind the Queen wearing gold turbans. But though their job was to wait on her, they were soon instructed to cook curries for Queen Victoria.

In the kitchen at Osborne House, the two servants would prepare the Queen's favourite Indian dishes, grinding fresh spices daily. Handwritten menus preserved at Osborne House show that Queen Victoria often enjoyed a chicken curry. Daal (written as dhal) was also a favourite. Unable to travel to India after she became Empress, she made sure that India came to Osborne House, and the Queen would have her Indian servants in full livery serve her in the garden or prepare a curry for her and her guests. The two Indian servants in fact became rather unpopular with the rest of the regular chefs as they cornered a part of the kitchen to do their daily grinding and roasting of spices, specially ordered by Her Majesty.

Such was the Queen's fascination with India that she wanted to re-create a mini India at Osborne. With Karim's help she employed an Indian architect and redesigned the living-room in white marble with Indian carvings and lattice-work and called it the Durbar Hall. It was here that she received her visitors while at her beloved Osborne and here that the royal family performed Christmas plays, with Munshiji and the other Indian servants often being given walk-on roles. Recently, to celebrate Queen Victoria's centenary, the Durbar Hall was painstakingly restored to its original splendour by English Heritage and today displays all the gifts received by Queen Victoria from her Indian subjects to mark the diamond jubilee of her reign.

During his tour of India in 1877, Prince Albert was supposed to have been motivated to visit the Madras Curry Club solely by a desire to taste their madras prawn curry. He was so impressed that, on his return, the chef on board the *Seraphis*, Monsieur Bonnemain, was given some lessons by the Indian cooks. But the Prince was disappointed with his French chef. He recorded:

the French intelligence, fine and keen as it is, does not penetrate the depths of curry lore, and the dishes, even after a considerable experience in the arts and sciences of several gentlemen of colour engaged expressly to dress curries never came up to the Indian standard.

Edward VII did not inherit Prince Albert's taste for curry but George V was the other extreme. He ate a curry for lunch every day and cared for little else.

One of the first known recipes for 'currey' is from Hannah Glasse's *Art of Cookery* in 1747. She mentions a chicken fricassee spiced with turmeric, ginger, and pepper 'beat very fine'. In 1772 the author of *The Complete Housekeeper and Professed Cook* also told how to make 'curry the Indian way'.

By 1773 curry had become the speciality of one London coffee house (the Coffee House in Haymarket). From about 1780 the first commercial curry powders were already on sale. While the English in India would rarely have used curry powder since they had a retinue of servants to grind the masala daily, the English back home no doubt considered curry powder a boon. The housewife often resorted to the curry powder as the mortars and pestles in the West were too lightweight to do justice to grinding such hard spices as fenugreek, poppy seeds, etc.

In his *Cook's Oracle* (1817), Dr Kitchiner had a recipe for curry powder boasting that 'the flavour approximates to the Indian powder so exactly, the most profound Palaticians have pronounced it a perfect copy of the original curry stuff'.

Apart from curry powder the flow from India of bottled sauces, chutneys and relishes continued throughout the eighteenth and nineteenth centuries. Returning nabobs brought them to England and so did those returning from civil and military service in India in the nineteenth century.

Gradually the meals served at English homes in India started evolving. The opening of the Suez Canal in 1869 led to another development in the culinary history of the subcontinent. Goods and ideas from Europe now speedily arrived in India and along with them the Victorian fashion for French cuisine. Another factor now entered Indian life – the memsahibs, wives of army officers or civil servants posted to India and also a large contingent of single women on the lookout for eligible men in India.

A new era of fusion foods was to begin, with the memsahib experimenting with her Indian cook and creating a variety of new dishes combining east and west. Before the arrival of the memsahib, the single Englishmen were happy to eat what their male servants prepared for them, which was usually traditional Indian food. Now the kitchen took on a new turn as the discerning memsahib left her stamp on the household and dictated the cuisine. The Mutiny and the establishment of the Raj produced a sea change in attitudes in India. To 'go native' was frowned upon and French food became favoured as the last word in sophistication and good taste.

What used to be the heavy lunch-time spread of Eliza Fay was substituted a century later by a lighter midday meal. About 1910, a suggested lunch consisted of pea soup, roast chicken and tongue, bread sauce, potatoes, cheese macaroni and lemon pudding. The main meal had moved to 7 or 8 p.m. In 1909 the writer Maud David declared that 'India is the land of dinners, as England is the land of five o'clock teas . . . all India is in a chronic state of giving and receiving (this) form of hospitality'.

The food evolving courtesy of the memsahibs brought to the table English-style soups, roasts, baked pies and puddings. The Indian ambience could not be avoided and was always absorbed. Fusion cooking evolved between the lady of the house and her Indian cook. Dishes like Windsor soup, Patna rice, a broth of doll (daal), Burdwan stew, cabobs, fish moley, curry, chutney and the famous Byculla soufflé were created in the heat and dust of the Indian kitchen.

Sir John Malcolm, who succeeded Monstuart Elphinstone as Governor of Bombay in 1827, wrote 'the only difference between Monstuart and me is that I have mulligatawny at tiffin (lunch) which comes of my experience at Madras', whereas the latter lunched on 'a few sandwiches and figs and a glass of water'.

Along with Anglo-Indian cuisine came a string of Anglo-Indian terms in the area of food. Punch was from *Paanch* (Hindi for five) and denoted the five components used in making the drink. Toddy came from the Hindi *tari* for the fermented sap of the tala or Palmyra palm. The peg as a measure of liquor got its name, according to the British humorists, because each one was a peg in one's coffin. Rice *congee*, an invalid's beverage, was the Tamil kanji, a translucent liquid which was also used by the washerman as an accessible source of starch for stiffening cotton clothes. Kedgeree for breakfast was the Hindi *khichri*, which visitors like Ibn Batuta in 1340 and Abdur Razzak in 1443 describe as a dish of rice cooked with *daal*, usually made from *moong*.

Rice cakes, *appa* or *appam* in Tamil, appeared at an English breakfast as *hoppers*: this was a word particularly used in Sri Lanka. Pepper water (*rasam*) was literally rendered into English as mulligatawny, a fiery soup. The baking of meat in a seal of dough, *dumpukht*, meaning air-cooled in Persian, and mentioned along with a recipe in the Ain-I-Akbari, became *dumpoke*, frequently applied to a dish of boned and stuffed duck. And, of course, the most famous Anglo-Indian term was *curry*, used to mean liquid broth, a thicker stew, or even a dry dish.

The moley was a corruption of the word *Malay*, perhaps indicative of its origin, and is a wet dish, which the British adopted, from Tamil Nadu with plenty of coconut. And there was the famous 'tiffin', the present late-afternoon snack meal of south India. Originally the word stood for the Anglo-Indian luncheon, and surprisingly its origin was not Indian at all. The word derives from both the slang English noun 'tiffing', for eating or drinking between meal times, and from the verb 'to tiff' which was to eat the midday meal. When dinner became a heavy evening meal, only a light snack was customary, which explains why the word tiffin appears only as late as 1807 in Anglo-Indian writings.

In the early nineteenth century, retired East Indian Company officials started a fashion for mulligatawny back in England. The soup now began to be further modified for the English kitchen: the mango juice of the Indian recipes was substituted by apple, and curry powder was used instead of the fresh spice mixture. The recipe began to be dubbed as 'curry soup'. Dr Kitchiner makes a mention of it in his *The Cook's Oracle*:

Mullaga-tawny signifies Pepper Water. The progress of the inexperienced peripatetic Palaticians has lately been arrested by these outlandish words being pasted on the windows of our Coffee Houses; it has we believe answered the 'restaurateur's purpose' and often excited JOHN BULL to walk in and taste:– the more familiar name of Curry Soup – would, perhaps, not have had sufficient of the charms of novelty to seduce him from his much-loved MOCK TURTLE. It is a fashionable soup and a great favourite with our East Indian friends.

Tins of mulligatawny paste also began to appear on shop shelves in the middle of the century, an indicator of how popular the soup had become.

Another popular creation of the Anglo-Indian kitchen was the kedgeree, derived from the Indian khichri, and still popular in Britain today. The original Indian khichri was a dish of daal and rice boiled together with spices such as coriander, cardamom, ginger and chilli. When the British arrived in the seventeenth century, they ate khichri as a breakfast dish, substituting flaked fish for the daal. Over time this was further modified and hard-boiled eggs were added. The spices were also modified or dropped, and soon the Anglo-Indian kedgeree was born.

Like mulligatawny, the recipe for kedgeree soon travelled back to England, and Scotland in particular where smoked fish – usually haddock – was used. The Victorian and Edwardian era saw kedgeree take a permanent place on any gentleman's country house breakfast table. Bertie Wooster once remarked, 'We really had breakfast . . . fried eggs, scrambled eggs, fishcakes and kedgeree, sometimes mushrooms, sometimes kidneys.'

One of the most colourful and entertaining cookery writers of Raj India was Colonel Kenney Herbert who famously wrote his *Culinary Jottings for Madras* in 1878. Herbert spent thirty-two years as a cavalry officer in southern India in Secunderabad, Bangalore and later Madras. Under the pen name of Wyvern he wrote a series of articles for the *Madras Mail* which subsequently became his famous book *Culinary Jottings*. He noted that, with the change in mood towards the natives after the Mutiny, curry had been banished from the dinner tables. He wrote:

For although a well-considered curry, or mulligatani – capital things in their way – are still very frequently given at breakfast or at luncheon, they no longer occupy a position in the dinner menu of establishments conducted according to the new regime.

The emphasis now was on French cooking which was considered fashionable and elegant, and menu cards would now have the fare in native French.

Colonel Herbert was quite critical of this pretentiousness and said the French fare turned out by the Indian cooks fell short of classic French cuisine. He returned to England at the turn of the century and such was his love for Indian food that he set up a cookery school in London and established himself as a cookery writer producing five more best-selling books: *Fifty Breakfasts*, *Fifty Luncheons*, *Fifty Dinners*, *Vegetarian and Simple Diet* and *Commonsense Cookery*. The Commonsense Cookery Association in London that he set up in Sloane Street had a cookery school attached and taught many an English housewife how to make the perfect curry.

Another popular writer of the day was Flora Annie Steel, who arrived in India in 1867 and established herself as an educationist. She published *The Complete Indian Housekeeper and Cook* which earned her the reputation of being the Mrs Beeton of British India. The book was hugely successful, running into ten editions.

It was the fictional account of an English officer's life in the mofussils (provincial districts) written by an army engineer, George Franklin Atkinson, that proved another bestseller. *Curry and Rice on Forty Plates* sketched a fictional picture of life in the English outposts in mofussil India. The book conjures up images of mess menus and open-air picnics and camps where the curry was prepared in an open pot.

For those returning from India in the nineteenth century and hankering for their curry in England, the only solution was to cook it themselves. For this there were already quite a few recipe books and orders for the spices had to be placed through the chemist.

The Wellcome Institute of the History of Medicine in London has some of the earliest recipes of curry powder recorded by English housewives. Mrs Turnbull's (first name not known) handwritten recipes for curry powder and Indian dishes date from 1820 to 1840 and include a collection of recipes and homemade medicinal decoctions made from Indian spices and herbs.

Her first recipe for curry powder contained the following ingredients:

6 oz turmeric
4 oz coriander seeds
2 oz cumin seeds
½ oz white pepper
¼ oz cayenne pepper
½ oz caraway seeds
½ oz ginger powder
2 oz fenugreek

Mrs Turnbull's recipes, written at 57 Queen's Garden, Hyde Park, probably after she returned from India, also included those for chutney, pilau, and ginger candy. There is a recipe for Indian pickle and the humble daal broth – described as being 'very good'.

Many of her recipes for curry powder were in bulk and one of them was enough to fill fifteen pint-size bottles, showing just how fond the Turnbulls were of their curry.

A second curry powder recipe from October 1827 is specifically described as being different in origin as it is mustard based. By this time all the ingredients – sarson, dhania, haldee, lal mirchee, etc. – are described in their original Hindustani showing familiarity with the usage.

There is also Mrs Horne's curry (a three-page detailed recipe for making meat curries) and Mrs Henry Woods's chicken curry. The latter two were probably friends who exchanged recipes. There are also recipes for Colonel R.'s curry, which is described as being very innovative with apples and broccoli and curds, and for lobster curry.

On 23 April 1844, Mrs Turnbull made another entry in her kitchen folder. She described it as yet 'another excellent recipe for curry powder'. It read:

best turmeric 1 lb
coriander seeds ¾ lb
ginger 3 lb
black pepper 2 lb
red pepper 2 lb

cardamom seeds ½ lb
caraway seeds ½ lb
60 cloves

Mix all the ingredients together and powder. Put into stoppered bottle. Two teaspoons are enough for curry for 5–6 people.

She also had details of where to obtain it: 'This can be made up at Beeces Medical Hall, Piccadilly, and the whole recipe will not cost more than seven shillings and is enough to last a family 5–6 months allowing *a curry for every day* [italics mine].' She also described the curry powder as an excellent seasoning for soups, broils etc.

Mrs Turnbull and her friends, Mrs Horne and Mrs Henry Woods, could not have imagined in their wildest dreams that the curry powder would transform the British kitchen 150 years on. Those who had returned to Blighty in the nineteenth century were already hankering for their curry and chemists' shops kept up a regular supply of curry powders. It was to be another century before the food would be available on every high street in Britain, fully cooked, prepared and served with complete Raj nostalgia.

2

The Street Where It All Began

In 1965 Muhammad Ali, an immigrant from Pakistan, decided to set up a sweet shop in London. He chose Drummond Street, a narrow street just behind Euston station. The shop was a small one on the first floor and Ali himself sat over a fire and made traditional jalebis, barfis and other Indian sweets. That was the beginning of Ambala Sweets, London's oldest sweet shop, and a name very much on the map even today.

Below Ambala was London's first halal restaurant, which has since closed down, and below the restaurant in the basement was a mosque. The local population of the area consisted mainly of Bangladeshi and Pakistani immigrants and Drummond Street soon became the place to eat, shop and talk subcontinent. Ambala's fame spread quickly and London's Indians from as far away as Southall and Wembley started converging on Drummond Street.

At Diwali and Dassehra, the queues were lengthy, stretching practically to the station. Muhammad became busier as the number of immigrants increased and Ambala and Drummond

27

Street became the destination before all festivals and functions. No story on Indian food can start without a visit to Drummond Street, the place where it all began.

The street itself was named after Lady Caroline Drummond, daughter of Kenneth Mackenzie, the sixth Earl of Seaforth, and wife of Louis Malcolm Drummond, the comte de Melfort. Were she to walk down Drummond Street today she would no doubt have a comment or two to make about the exotic sounding names of the shops and restaurants on the street. On one side of the rather narrow drab street stands Gupta Sweets, a branch of the famous sweet shop from India, and next to it an Indian vegetable and grocery shop. A few shops away is the Ambala Sweet Centre, with its gleaming window-display of colourful sweets, looking no different from a sweet shop in a bustling part of Delhi's Chandni Chowk or Karol Bagh areas. A proud sign outside the shop says it was established in 1965.

A few shops away from Ambala is the tastefully decorated Chutneys vegetarian restaurant, where one can usually see queues just before lunch or dinner for their famous eat-as-much-as-you-like buffets. Chutneys was built in 1987 on the site of one of London's oldest Indian restaurants and a Drummond Street favourite – Shahs. On the opposite side is one of London's oldest and most popular vegetarian restaurants, Diwana Bhelpuri House, and a few doors away, another vegetarian favourite, the Ravi Shankar restaurant.

The non-vegetarian restaurants of the area – the Raavi Kebab Halal Tandoori, the Haandi and the Shah Tandoori – offer standard curry-house fare. Raavi Kebab has on its menu a rich haleem. It has been an established name in Drummond Street for the past two decades and is patronised by the local Asians. But Drummond Street is famous for its vegetarian restaurants and sweet shops rather than the non-vegetarian restaurants.

That the local population is heavily Bangladeshi is evident from the shop-window signs, which are often in Bengali. A travel agent sells cheap tickets to Dhaka, a local grocery shop sells exotic vegetables imported from Bangladesh such as raw jackfruit, banana flowers, Bengal beans, Bengal spinach and fiery green chillies. And where there are Bengalis there is fish. The shops on Drummond Street sell hilsa, rui, papda, bhetki and other river fish flown in twice a week directly from Bangladesh. A shop selling Islamic books, and a mosque around the corner, would no doubt convince Lady Caroline that she was in the wrong country.

Sandwiched between the sweets, samosas and fish is a collection of New Age and hippy shops. Sitting beside the Indian shops, and in fact blending in with what after all was derived from Oriental mysticism, are the remnants of the flower-power age. On sale are sixties and seventies memorabilia which are currently enjoying a revival. The shops under the mystic maze banner sell everything from incense to crystal mobiles,

29

beads and baubles, books on meditation and yoga, music and clothes.

To add to the diversity of the area there is also an African crafts shop. The mystic shops offer things from the Far East, Africa and Latin America, while the Indian shops provide the best snacking after the shopping.

It was here in Drummond Street that some of the biggest names in the Indian food business made their humble beginnings. It was a few doors away from Ambala at 134 Drummond Street that the Pathaks set up their first shop in 1958. Today the Pathaks are virtually the first family of Indian food business, with their famous pastes and pickles stocked in every supermarket, corner shop and grocery store from the Scottish Highlands to the Cornish coast.

Fresh from Kenya as a refugee in 1956, Lakhubhai Pathak, his wife Shanta Gauri and son Kirit worked 18 hours a day making samosas in a 5 × 6ft kitchen to survive. Slowly contracts came from the Indian High Commission and various other Indian organisations for private functions. Finally Lakhubhai managed to save enough to buy a shop in Drummond Street and the famous street acquired its first and most famous Indian resident.

The Pathaks sold not just samosas and bhajis, but also pickles, Indian spices, papads and fresh vegetables. Lakhubhai became the first person in London to start importing fresh vegetables from India and east Africa. Soon Indians could buy bhindi, tindora, turia, dhania, green chillies, etc.

all at Pathak's store in Drummond Street. The ethnic shops in Wembley and Southall today, which are spilling over with Indian vegetables imported from India and Kenya, are doing what Lakhubhai Pathak began doing on a small scale over thirty years ago.

Industrialist Lord Paul remembers even today how he used to visit Lakhubhai Pathak's shop when he had just arrived in London in 1966 for his daughter's treatment:

We used to live fairly close by in Portland Place, and Lakhubhai Pathak's shop was the only place we could go to buy Indian spices, pickles and vegetables. He was always very welcoming and friendly as well. Soon the whole street began to buzz with life, Indian shops, restaurants. It had a wonderful atmosphere and made every Indian feel at home.

There was more to come. By 1972, a professional Bombay cyclist who was missing his native Chowpatti Beach decided to set up a restaurant selling beach snacks on Drummond Street. Jayant Shah, a member of the Indian cycling team left India on a world tour and never went back to Bombay. His father was a teacher and his three brothers were professionals, but Jayant Shah always had a spirit of adventure and went in for a career in sports. It was on one of the cycling trips that he went to Poland in 1949 where he met his future wife. Jayant married in 1958 and transferred to London. For a few years he worked as a manager in two Indian vegetarian restaurants and finally started Diwana Bhelpuri House in 1972.

What Jayant Shah wanted to do was to introduce *bhelpuri* to London, a snack he had been missing sorely since his Bombay days. The Shahs had lived near Chowpatty in Bombay and Jayant practically grew up on bhelpuri. A café called Jo's Café was on sale in Drummond Street and Jayant Shah put all his savings together, borrowed the rest, and bought his first place on Drummond Street. It was Drummond Street's first vegetarian restaurant.

His son, Chris Patel, who ran the restaurant until 1999, remembered how the first café opened with four tables and a small kitchen with his father himself cooking. One day it rained and the kitchen roof started leaking. His father simply carried on cooking, holding an umbrella over his head, frying dosas and bhajis as if nothing in the world could stop him.

Ironically, in the first week business was so bad that Jayant Shah took his week's takings to the bookies and gambled it. He then leased the ground floor and moved the kitchen to the basement.

Under Jayant Shah's enterprise, Diwana Bhelpuri House, soon became the most famous Indian vegetarian restaurant in London. It won numerous awards and was listed by the *Evening Standard* as one of London's best Indian vegetarian restaurants. Other listings followed in *Time Out – Eating Out in London, The Good Food*

Guide, Egon Ronay's *Just a Bite*, Sarah Brown's *Guide to Vegetarian London* and in *City Limits*. Diwana, a restaurant selling masala dosa and bhelpuri even made it to the pages of *Vogue*.

Diwana's plus points were its natural stripped wooden walls and wooden benches, simple menus, lack of fuss and its air of no-nonsense professionalism. For Londoners bored with tandoori and tikkas, Jayant Shah's Chowpatty Beach menu was a pleasant break. Here one could have bhelpuri, dahi wada, samosas, masala dosas and filling vegetarian thalis, all for a fraction of the price paid at other restaurants.

Soon Drummond Street became the Mecca of vegetarian restaurants and quickly earned the name of Little Bombay. Taking their cue from Diwana came two more veggie restaurants, Ravi Shankar and Chutneys, both serving food similar to Diwana, and all becoming immediately popular with the critics and clients though Diwana, the oldest, always had the edge on the rest.

Chris Patel, who was a little boy when his father started Diwana, remembers the atmosphere as it used to be in those early days in the seventies:

It was completely different to what it is now. Then it was like a big family. The first generation bonded well. They were all fresh from India and Pakistan, determined to succeed in a foreign country. There was also the feeling that they had come from a newly independent country, there was a sense of pride.

'There were no differences and no rivalries between the Indians and the Pakistanis either,' said Chris. 'In this country they were all from the subcontinent, and that's what mattered. The old wounds of Partition had been left behind and the main aim was to establish themselves in Britain.'

So while Ambala's owners came from Pakistan, Jayant Shah was from Bombay and the Pathaks were Indians from Kenya. It was a rich multicultural mix and the families got along well.

None of us lived in the area, but we all used to come on weekends and sometimes after school. I used to help in the shop. My father genuinely believed in customer service, so he would mix with all the guests and see they were well looked after. . . . Drummond Street then was something like Covent Garden and Leicester Square are now. There used to be jugglers and artists performing on the street. There was always something going on. It was constantly like a carnival.

Chris remembered how Diwana Bhelpuri House was like a meeting place for those from India: 'Most of the people who would come here knew each other. They would meet at the tables and talk, and remember their days in India or Kenya. I often recognised the faces, though I was quite young then.'

A day at Drummond Street for any Indian would inevitably be a shopping spree and a stock-up session at Pathak's store, followed by tea and snacks at Diwana and a last stopover at Ambala to buy some sweets to take home.

The owner of another famous Drummond Street store, Gupta Sweets, Jagdish Gupta remembers how the rich Sindhi Indian ladies used to drive up in their Mercedes and go shopping on Drummond Street in the early seventies and eighties: 'Everything that you wanted from India was there, and everybody converged there.'

Gupta Sweets, the famous sweet shop chain from east India (the Gupta brothers' sweet shop in Calcutta is run by a relative), with its Calcutta-style sandesh and rajbhog sweets, opened in Drummond Street in 1983. Jagdish Gupta remembers how Lakhubhai Pathak used to sit in his shop making jalebis once a week. He, like all the other Drummond Street residents, thought the atmosphere was wonderful.

To add to the ethnic diversity of Drummond Street, Jagdish Gupta came from Gaya in Bihar. In his shop hangs a photograph of their famous sweet shop started by his grandfather near the Bishnupad temple in Gaya and then run by his father Raghu Nandan Prasad Gupta. The Gupta family were traditional sweet-makers or halwais and it was this expertise that made the shop one of the most sought-after on Drummond Street.

Jagdish Gupta came to London in 1957 after graduating from Gaya University. Setting up a sweet shop was the last thing on his mind. Instead Jagdish Gupta wanted to have an import–export business in mica, the famous mineral from Bihar. But after a few years when the mica business was not doing well, he decided to go back to his old family trade. Taking advantage of the Labour government's immigration policy of 1979, he managed to bring a cook from Bihar. That year they started their first sweet shop on the site of the old mica business office in Hendon in north-west London. But Drummond Street, he knew, was the place to be. One day he noticed a 'To Let' sign outside a shop there. It was the last day for application. Jagdish Gupta's nephew rushed to submit the application and in a few days they received a call from the agents. The shop started trading soon after that, though the Guptas had to deal with some initial hostility from the old monopolists of Drummond Street, Ambala.

But the quality and range of sweets was different and soon everything settled down again in Drummond Street. Gupta Sweets specialised in sandesh, rasmalai and special Bengali sweets like kheer kadam, pure pista barfi and almond barfi. Even the samosas at Gupta had a different taste and were closer to the Bengali singara then the north Indian samosa served in Ambala and Diwana. They also specialised in Bengali kochuris and on special orders made Bengali vegetable chops. The clientele for Guptas were inevitably the Bengalis of London, most of whom were already familiar with the branches of Gupta Brothers in India. Apart from the Gupta Brothers in Chetla in Calcutta, the extended Gupta family own the Ram

Bhandar in Varanasi and the Ram Ashray in Lucknow. The original sweet shop in Gaya still remains. But Jagdish Gupta is disillusioned with the condition of Drummond Street. It has lost its vibrancy and the people are not so friendly any more, he says. 'It is not the community it used to be,' he regrets.

Until recently, the frequent occurrence of small crimes and violence between local Bangladeshi youths and white youths made the area unpopular and run-down. Competition from shops in Wembley and Southall also led to a slump in business in Drummond Street.

In 1993, an eleven-year-old English boy, Richard Everitt, was murdered by a gang of Bangladeshi youths barely one and a half miles from Drummond Street. It was apparently a revenge killing. Everitt was an innocent schoolboy who got caught in the crossfire between white and Bangladeshi youths. The event sparked an immediate outcry as it was the first killing of a white youth by an Asian gang.

There was much talk in the media of second-generation militant Bangladeshi youths who would not put up with racist attacks as their elders had. In 1993 there had been a spate of attacks on Bangladeshi youths in east London and none of the assailants were arrested. Richard Everitt, cycling along his housing estate, was not fast enough to avoid his attackers and paid the price for the previous senseless attacks on the Bangladeshi youths.

As the whole area from Kings Cross to east London became tense, the effect could be felt in Drummond Street as well. Business was affected, and the evening crowds normally milling at Diwana and Chutney came to a virtual standstill. 'Nobody wanted to come this way, specially in the evening,' said Chris Patel. 'The only people coming in were lunchtime office-goers. It took a long time to recover from that.'

But Chris Patel said it was never the same at Drummond Street again. He sold off his shop in 1999 following ill-health:

Now most of the people visiting Diwana are white, those who work or live in the area or those who have heard of the restaurant and come specially to eat there. The growth of Indian eating houses in Wembley and Southall means that not many Indians need to come here any more when they can eat locally in their own area. I live in Wembley myself and when I had my van with Diwana Bhelpuri House written on it parked outside, people would come up to me and say, 'Ah, we used to go there once. We don't go much now.' So it was one of the ironies of having more competition here.

Diwana describes its peak period as the late seventies and early eighties. That was the time the awards were flowing, business was flourishing and Diwana was well known on the London food map.

Jayant Shah died in 1986, a year after his wife. She had never really taken to Indian food and used to work in a north London café, not involving herself much with her husband's restaurant. Chris and his sister, brought up as Roman Catholics, learnt the restaurant trade from their father. They managed the café until recently, retaining the old menu which always remained the most popular. When they sold up, it ended another era in Drummond Street.

The café, under new management, is still popular, but the old residents feel the buzz has definitely gone. Chris pointed out that all the shops on Drummond Street now have shutters, something they never had previously. Crime and violence has gone up, pushing Drummond Street downmarket and turning it into a typical inner-city area; a far cry from the days when Jayant Shah, Muhammad Ali and Lakhubhai Pathak opened their shops on the same street.

Camden Council, the local council in charge of the area, has now taken steps to ensure that the area is cleaned up, well patrolled and crime taken care of. The council is also taking steps to make the place prettier, more eye-catching and better signposted in the next few years. The council has been criticised by local shopkeepers for failing to give the area the publicity it deserves and has taken note of the complaints. Better lighting, better pavements, trees, flowers are all in the pipeline to transform Drummond Street and put it firmly on the tourist map: a welcome step, for it was here in the heart of London, easily accessible from the West End, that Indian shops and restaurants first made their mark. Similar eating houses have now spread to the suburbs – in Wembley and Southall – but Drummond Street will always remain the famous name it was: the street where you could find the multicultural buzz of the subcontinent combining Bombay snacks with Calcutta sweets, the famous Pathak pastes from Kenya and Gujarat, delicious kebabs from Pakistan and fresh fruit and vegetables from Bangladesh. 'Doing a Drummond' would mean tasting the best of all these regions and a guaranteed great day out; but that was in the seventies and early eighties. The story of Indian food in Britain was to develop and the curry map would slowly grow bigger.

3

Curries on Shelves –
the Supermarket Story

As Indian cuisine started gaining in popularity during the eighties, it was time for the food to start entering the supermarkets. The growth of the supermarket shopping culture in Britain went side by side with the demand for Indian food. One will have to look at Britain's shopping ethos to understand how the presence of Indian food on supermarket shelves simply kept on growing.

Ask the average Briton what he does on weekends or his spare time and he will probably say shopping. The Saturday-morning jams at shopping centres say it all: the British are compulsive shoppers. Whether it is walking the high streets searching for the season's latest fashions, or browsing around electronic stores, furniture centres and DIY shops, there is always something to lure the shopper. To cope with the demand, shops are now staying open on Sundays, sacrificing the traditional family-day in.

Battling with the supermarket trolley is very much part of the British weekend. The corner shop is being outdone by the supermarket that offers under one roof groceries, electronics, clothes, music, dry-cleaning and, most attractively, free parking. 'Have trolley, will fill,' say psychologists, and as the consumer stocks up simply because he sees an object on the shelf, the supermarkets rake in the profits.

All the supermarkets – Sainsbury's, Tesco, Safeway, Asda, Waitrose, to name but a few – stock a large variety of Indian meals and most of them say their Indian range is the fastest selling of the chilled meals and the most popular. All the supermarkets are trying their best to increase the variety, adding new dishes every year and headhunting the best Indian chefs for the job.

Not only are the supermarkets offering the ready-cooked meals, they are stocking their shelves with a wide variety of pastes, pickles and curry powders. Previously most people looking for Indian food ingredients – daals, rice, spices – had to go to an Indian shop to buy them. Now they can be spoilt for choice at their own local Sainsbury's or Asda. On offer is everything from the raw material to the finished product. Indian vegetables like karela, bhindi, dudhi, green chillies, coriander, curry leaves, fill the shelves, as do daals and spices, pickles and pastes. There is even a choice of brands on offer. You can go for the ethnic spice suppliers like Natco and Rajah or opt for Sharwood's and Uncle Ben's. Most supermarkets do their own brand of curry pastes as well.

Competition is fierce and Patak's – the original pickle and paste company – now finds it has to fight for space on supermarket shelves with a whole range of ethnic paste manufacturers, from Geeta's, Rajahs and the Tilda–Madhur Jaffrey range to the established non-ethnic big brands such as Sharwood's and Uncle Ben's. Everyone, it seems, wants a piece of the spice cake.

One of Britain's oldest retailers is Sainsbury's which changed the face of food-retailing in Britain with its supermarkets and hypermarkets. Sainsbury's opened its first shop in Drury Lane in London's Covent Garden in 1869. At a time in Victorian England, when most grocery shops still covered the floors with sawdust, Sainsbury's had tiled interiors and staff dressed in starched white aprons. The first store was a small dairy and soon its reputation for cleanliness and uniformed staff who gave friendly over-the counter service grew. Sainsbury's opened Britain's first self-service supermarket in 1954, heralding a new age in supermarkets. Today the family empire has expanded to over 200 stores up and down the country.

Sainsbury's Indian chilled meal section is extremely popular and the store emphasises that it is using genuine freshly ground spices. Noon Products, based in Southall in West London, are the suppliers to Sainsbury's. The supermarket serves around forty varieties of meal including the famous chicken tikka masala, chicken korma and chicken vindaloo. Sainsbury's launched Indian meals in 1989 and now has a sophisticated range of dishes covering the various regions of India. It has gone into previously uncharted areas like the cuisine of Bengal – Bengali mustard chicken and Bengali pilau rice – and also the popular dishes from south India and the Konkan coast. These include Chettinad chicken, Kerala mango curry and piri piri chicken. From north India, it serves butter chicken: a much-favoured dish from Delhi and Punjab and a close cousin of the British chicken tikka masala.

Waitrose, the food arm of the John Lewis partnership, claims it was among the first to stock Indian chilled food which it started doing from 1987. It now sells nearly forty varieties of Indian chilled meals and includes such exotic treats as mango chicken, Goan fish curry and salmon piri piri. All supermarkets have started following the way in which customers order at restaurants – asking for starters, main courses and desserts – and now offer the complete range of all three. They have also started doing the popular Indian concept of thali – or a set meal – and provide takeaway packets of rice, naan, starters, a meat curry and a choice of vegetable dishes.

The supermarket chain Tesco is also a big player in the Indian food business, supplying over thirty varieties of Indian food and is well stocked with Indian spices and condiments. Asda, part of the American Wal-Mart supermarket chain, that became involved in a price war with Tesco, is also well up with the competition and has a large Indian selection of meals, spices and vegetables.

Safeway entered late in the race to fill the chilled counters with Indian food products

(1992–3), but it started a new trend in late night shopping by keeping its stores open until 10 p.m. and was one of the first to start Sunday opening. It serves popular dishes like tandoori chicken and has regional varieties like chicken balchao and Goan chicken.

What began as a few simple meals in the supermarkets, comprising chicken tikka masala, rogan josh and chicken curry, has evolved into a sophisticated range covering dishes from the various regions of India from Bengal to Kerala. All the supermarkets maintain, however, that chicken tikka masala remains one of their most popular dishes, and retain it on their menu.

The corporate affairs manager at Waitrose said that the consumer was becoming more sophisticated in his knowledge of Indian food and regional food was considered authentic and exciting. A similar view was echoed by Safeway. Marks & Spencer (M&S) felt that the British loved hot and spicy dishes and were ready to try new flavours.

M&S remains one of the most popular high-street department stores selling Indian food. M&S chilled meals are snapped up by shoppers on the high street and the Indian range has always been its most popular. M&S has frequent launches of its Indian food and at present provides a range of forty-five products.

The store researchers say that Britons simply cannot get enough spicy food and every new product is eagerly picked up by consumers and becomes a bestseller. To keep up with the competition from other stores to bring the newest authentic range of Indian food on the shelves, M&S launched a new range in October 2002 specially prepared by none other than Atul Kochhar, the Michelin-starred chef, formerly of the Tamarind restaurant. Some of the new dishes included marathi lamb shank – lamb on the bone that has been marinated in yoghurt and a blend of spices, and tandoori chicken cooked in a traditional tandoori for the authentic flavour.

The M&S statistics are awesome: the store declares that: 'As a nation we eat ten packs of M&S curry every minute of the day – that's enough portions in a year to give one to each of the nine million people who live in Bombay.' The store also concludes that:

- Britain's favourite Indian meal is chicken tikka masala – M&S sells 18 tons of it each week.
- M&S sells enough rice each year to tip 140 elephants off the scales.
- The curry suppliers to M&S use an astonishing three-quarters of a million garlic bulbs each year.
- If all the packs of M&S chicken tikka masala eaten in a year were laid end to end, they would stretch from London to Birmingham and back.
- M&S uses enough cream and yoghurt a week in its Indian dishes to fill an Olympic size swimming pool.

- The hotter the better is how the Brits like their curries – the fiery piri piri is a distinctive Goan recipe which is now one of the most popular produced by M&S.

M&S has closely followed the trend in English curry-eating habits. It has noted that in the seventies it was tandoori, in the eighties Britons were bowled over by balti, by the early nineties they were experimenting with regional curries and by the end of the nineties it was the haandi (slow cooked in a special copper or clay pot) range. The store concludes that curry remains king in a nation where one in eight adults is an Indian-food fanatic, as 2.5 million diners eat out in the over 8,000 Indian restaurants in the UK each week.

Most importantly, the store concludes that curry is addictive. Eating chillies releases endorphins, the body's natural painkillers, which give you a feel-good factor. So we eat more chilli because it makes us feel good.

When the Paris store of M&S closed down, the French moaned that they would not get their Indian meals any more, especially the chicken tikka sandwiches. The M&S Paris store used to sell more Indian dishes than any of its UK counterparts, showing that the French could be tempted with Indian food as well.

Behind M&S's popular Indian meal section was Shehzad Husain, the store's food consultant. Husain has now moved on and launched her own brand of curry pastes which are available at

Harvey Nichol's, but she was the person who made M&S curries famous.

Husain has an interesting story to tell about how she joined the store in the eighties. Pakistan-born Shehzad Husain came with her parents to England in her schooldays. Her father was a scientist and theirs was a middle-class family from Hyderabad with the familiar Hyderabadi cuisine being prepared in the home every day. Shehzad had no formal culinary qualifications and no ambitions to become a chef either. Instead she studied beauty culture at a London college and married a chartered accountant, eventually settling down to become a housewife and mother.

Her mother taught her the basic steps of cooking and Shehzad tried out the recipes in her family kitchen. By the early eighties when her children started going to school, Shehzad was able to publish a few recipes in cookery magazines and started teaching cookery at the Cordon Bleu School in London.

One day her mother brought home an M&S ready Indian meal and declared that it was 'awful rubbish, really hopeless'. She asked Shehzad to ring up M&S and tell them what she thought of their food and how it wasn't at all authentic and how she could do it better. Shehzad was hesitant at first, but her mother was insistent and she soon found herself calling the store. After a couple of meetings with M&S officials, Shehzad cooked the selectors lunch at her home. She was immediately offered the job of becoming a consultant on the company's Indian range. It was 1983 and with Shehzad now supervising, M&S withdrew the existing 'not very good' range. Nine months later Shehzad introduced her 'proper authentic' range containing fresh herbs and spices, since when there was no looking back.

M&S was very proud of Shehzad Husain and of the fact that an ordinary housewife joined their ranks and gave their products the ring of authenticity. She soon introduced a 26-dish range of curries to the store and began what was a minor revolution in supermarket curries. The haandi range of M&S curries included recipes which had been tucked away for years by Shehzad's family in Hyderabad.

Going for the authentic has been the benchmark with all the supermarkets. Teams from the supermarkets regularly visit India to catch up on the latest trends in cooking. In 2001, Sainsbury's sent a team to Goa and Kerala to check on exciting new dishes and came up with a whole new package of regional dishes. Meanwhile M&S went on a 'Tikka Tubby Tour' visiting the curry capitals of Britain looking at Indian restaurants in Birmingham, Bradford, Glasgow and Leicester to keep track of the latest dishes being demanded by the consumer and to spot new trends.

Neither is it just the stores in London or the Midlands – where a large number of the ethnic minority population live – that stock the curries. Stores up and down the country have filled their shelves with Indian meals and spices. Once, while

driving through the remote market town of
Caernarfon in North Wales, it was a pleasant
surprise to see a Safeway store well stocked with
Patak's vindaloo, korma pastes and pickles. Every
possible spice was also available in this small
Welsh coastal town where virtually the whole
population was white.

Again, on a cottage holiday in Carlisle in the
Lake District one year, we found a well-stocked
Tesco supermarket with a complete range of Indian
chilled meals, ready to heat and eat, perfect for the
slightly nippy late August weather.

Supermarkets have made life easy for the
working couple or single person. Chilled meals
picked up on the way home provide an easy
dinner on no-cooking nights. For those wanting to
cook for themselves, but be spared the hassle of
grinding the spices, curry pastes provide the
answer. Simply let Patak's, Sainsbury's, Tilda or
Sharwood's do it for you. The most you'll have to
do is chop an onion and stir in the paste with lamb
or chicken for an exotic Indian meal.

So popular are these pastes, that Meena Pathak
(the person behind Patak's pastes) says she has
seen her pastes selling in Bombay's Chor Bazar
(flea market). There are several Indians who take
back from England not just her pastes but her
pickles as well; talk about taking coals to
Newcastle. In fact, companies in India have seen
the market potential of curry pastes (housewives
and working women everywhere want hassle-free
cooking), and a range of these pastes is being

produced in India for the Indian market – another British invention that has travelled back to the land of its origin.

And if they are being taken even to India, why wouldn't the supermarkets in Britain stock up? For all those who want a curry-in-a-hurry, the supermarkets have provided all the options. As the shelves stacked with Indian products continue to grow, it's a sure sign that kormas and vindaloos are being stirred up in many British kitchens. Goodbye Oxo gravy cubes, welcome Patak's korma paste. Did someone say chillies were addictive?

4

The Very Pukka Pathaks

On a bleak industrial estate in the Lancashire town of Wigan, stands a modest building called Kiriana House. Behind the name is a family history, inside the double glass doors is the story of Britain's oldest Indian food family, the Pathaks. The products stand on a display shelf in the entrance lobby: a colourful, slickly packaged range of pickles, poppadoms, and pastes that is the Patak's hallmark. And in a glass case, neatly displayed, stands the past: old labels of Patak's pickles, a booklet containing a detailed product and price list of the first family store in London, and a recipe collection.

The place doesn't smell of curry powders and pastes for the factory is located five miles away. The head office is where the planning and development is done and from where the cans and tins of Patak's products make their way on heavy-duty trucks to shops and supermarkets all over the country.

Up the road from Kiriana House is the factory of Heinz, the multinational food manufacturers famous for their soups and baked beans. Once there were coal mines in the area, and George Orwell made it famous with his novel *The Road to Wigan Pier*. But there isn't really a pier, only a pub that enjoys the name. Now there aren't any coal mines either and the major employers are Heinz and Patak's. History tends to take some strange twists and turns.

The name of the Patak's office – Kiriana – is short for Kirit, Neeraj, Nayan, Anjali and Meena, the present and future owners of Patak's. Kiriana also means *kiraana* or grocery store, which is how the story of the £45 million company began.

It was in Keshod, a village in Gujarat, where Lakshmishankar Pathak, popularly known as Lakhubhai Pathak, was born in 1925. His father, Gopalshankar, was a poor subsistence farmer who had borrowed heavily to build a family house for his wife and six children from a second marriage. The farm income was insufficient to pay the debts and his father started a snack shop in the village selling sweets and savouries to supplement the family income. All the money was taken by loan sharks – the family income of two rupees equalled the interest of the loan also at two rupees – and life was tough for the Pathak family.

Lakshmishankar went to a local school, but education was never a priority and he had only read two books in school up to the age of ten. The daily family routine was helping their father in the shop and on the field. After his classes Lakshmishankar would deliver milk to earn some vital extra money.

But if things were bad, they only got worse. Lakshmishankar's father died suddenly when the boy was still just a child, and the future looked bleak for the family as the loan sharks surrounded them. Responsibility for the family fell on the shoulders of the eldest son, Dayashankar Pathak, who had to keep the family from starving. The British at that time were offering incentives to people to work in east Africa and the family abandoned their house in Keshod and set sail for Kenya.

Lakshmishankar was only ten at the time. The family landed in Kissumu in Kenya and started doing what they were good at: selling sweets and savouries. Dayashankar rented a shop and soon a familiar board went up outside: *Pathak's Sweets*. The family was in business again. After the poverty of India, Kenya seemed bliss. Business was good, the shop's reputation grew and soon there were queues outside.

There were quite a few Indians in Kenya and a market for the products existed. The family soon earned enough to pay off their debts in India and bought the shop rented by Dayashankar. Dayashankar soon had a large family – thirteen children of whom nine survived – and the family grew in size and prosperity. They bought a large house in Kissumu with extensive grounds and the whole family lived and worked together. Soon it was time for Lakshmishankar to get married and a bride was found for him from the local Indian community in Kenya. Shanta Gauri joined the Pathak family and soon the two had six children.

Although they were fairly wealthy and things were going well, Shanta Gauri started to become restless. The pressures of living in a large joint family were telling on her. Her brother-in-law's nine children and six of her own were a lot to handle even for her. She started telling Lakshmishankar to move out and do his own thing.

Meanwhile in the 1950s the political climate was changing in Kenya. The Mau Mau terror was causing insecurity among local Indians and there were many people who started talking of fleeing. At the shop, Shanta Gauri and Lakshmishankar heard other Indians talk about England and the charm and prosperity of the colonial power. One of his brothers had set up a business in the clothes trade and also brought back stories of prosperity outside Kenya. By now Shanta Gauri had heard enough and she told her husband that he was slaving in Kenya and not getting anything, so he must leave. Lakshmishankar made a first trip to England in 1953 and came back with a reasonably good impression of the country. As things worsened back home, he decided to try his luck and leave for England. When his elder brother heard his plans, he wanted to stop him. A family row followed and Lakshmishankar was told that if he left Kenya he would have to leave without a penny. Even his ticket would not be paid for by his brother. His in-laws lent him some money and Lakshmishankar took the decision to leave the family business. In 1956, the family of eight (with the six children aged between three and eleven) climbed on board the SS *Uganda* and set sail for England. Lakshmishankar had a little borrowed money, a life insurance policy that he wanted to encash, and nothing more. Kirit Pathak, the fourth child and present owner of Pataks, was then four years old.

It was the story of every immigrant: sitting on a ship with bag and baggage and dreaming ahead of a life of prosperity. Like all immigrants, the Pathak family was making a continuous westward journey. Lakshmishankar had been only ten when his brother had taken him from Gujarat to Kenya. There had also been six brothers and sisters on board the ship. Now here he was taking his six children to a new life in England. All that four-year-old son Kirit could remember of the journey was the swimming pool on the ship, surrounded by the vast ocean. After several weeks at sea, the ship docked in Marseilles, where it was going to wait for a few days.

Lakshmishankar jumped ship at Marseilles and decided to carry on ahead overland so that he could fix up a place to stay when the family arrived. In November 1956 he arrived on a train from Marseilles to London. By this time he was down to his last £5 and his insurance policy. No one wanted to rent him a house and he searched for several days in desperation.

Finally with the help of a character reference from the Kenyan branch of a UK bank, he was able to borrow some money, and rented a house in

Kentish Town in north London. 'I don't know what it was that made this bank manager give the money,' said Meena Pathak, his daughter-in-law. 'Maybe he just had a feeling that this man would achieve something.'

Lakshmishankar Pathak rented the semi-detached house and went to receive his family. 'He welcomed us at Tilbury Docks,' recalls Kirit Pathak. 'And we walked with our suitcases from Chalk Farm tube station to our new home, new country and new life.'

Once the family was safely settled in at home, Lakshmishankar put on his only suit and went out immediately to search for a job. But there was nothing at that time for an illiterate immigrant. For days he knocked at several doors and finally in desperation he walked into the offices of Camden Council and said he would take anything. They gave him a job cleaning the sewers.

For an orthodox Brahmin, it was the ultimate insult. But he swallowed his pride and cleaned the drains. The family had to be fed and there was nothing that could be done. But his wife was a proud woman and couldn't bear the thought of her husband doing menial work. 'We were better off with the Mau Mau,' she would cry. The family had been fairly prosperous when they had left Kenya and the degradation was too much to take. But Shanta Gauri was not one to give up easily. She sold what jewellery she had left and bought some second-hand pots and pans. If this was to be the new life, she would have to get things going.

Having encouraged her husband to move to the West, she now told him the best way forward: do what you do best, do what you know, she told him. It was back to the karahi and back to the sweets and savouries business.

Like his uncle before him in Kenya, Lakhubhai Pathak too picked up the karahi as the sole means of providing for his family, and settled down in his London kitchen to churn out what he was traditionally good at. The entire family helped. From the tiny kitchen in Kentish Town came samosas, bhajis, gathias, and other snacks and sweets that the Indian palate loved. Lakhubhai Pathak was then about twenty-five years old.

Lakhubhai's first customers were Indian students. A lot of students studying medicine and law lived around the area, in digs or as paying guests. All of them missed home-cooked Indian food. Always a generous and impulsive man, Lakhubhai started playing host to the students, calling them over for free meals. Soon the word spread, and what Meena Pathak calls London's first takeaway service was in operation:

And it was operating right there from this Kentish Town house serving the Indian students. Kirit's mum was constantly slaving over the stove making the meals, while Lakhubhai was calling all the students over to come and get a meal.

But the initial sales skills worked. Soon the students wanted to pay for the service. They realised Lakhubhai had six children and needed the money. The Pathaks' fame spread by word of mouth and soon a regular supply system was working. The family worked 18 hours a day slaving over a hot stove. When the children came back from school they helped as well. It was a sweatshop, but the Pathaks were doing what they were best at. And it was better any day than cleaning sewers, according to Meena:

It was the right time and the right place . . . God had a part to play in it. This was the time that there were a lot of Indian students. But more importantly, the British were gradually coming back from India. And they were returning with a taste for Indian food, which they had got used to. Here was the chance to give them what they missed.

The family chipped in doing their bit. Kirit's elder brother would go on a bike selling the snacks and delivering them. Kirit – who could travel free on trains – would also do deliveries. From his parents, Kirit learnt to make pedas and jalebis and the sons soon learnt the skills.

Meanwhile Lakhubhai had started catering for functions at the Indian High Commission. The diplomats in India House were delighted when Lakhubhai visited them with samples, since no one was cooking such traditional food in those days.

In 1958 he won his first big contract to cater for the Queen's Garden Party at Buckingham Palace. He also supplied snacks for a reception hosted by Lord Mountbatten, which made him very proud.

Meanwhile, as business was steadily picking up, Lakhubhai decided his sons must not be denied the education he never had. Four of them – Kirit and three of his brothers and sisters – were packed off, with a loan from his brother in Italy, to a Roman Catholic boarding school in southern Ireland.

The children spent five years in boarding school and Kirit even went on to become an altar boy. On one of his vacations, young Kirit shocked his devoutly Hindu dad by saying that he wanted to become the Pope.

In 1958, with business expanding, Lakhubhai managed to gather enough funds to buy his first shop in Drummond Street in Euston. The street became famous because of the Pathaks' shop and gradually the area came to be known as 'Little Bombay'. The tiny premises on 135 Drummond Street now sported a familiar sign: Pathak's (Spices) Ltd. Lakhubhai had made it this far. The shop soon had a huge clientele – from students to businessmen – and sold everything that was needed in an Indian home, from fresh vegetables to spices and *hawan samagri* (items needed for Hindu religious ceremonies) to frying pans.

The Pathaks became the first people to import fresh vegetables into the UK and soon there were long queues outside the shop. Behind the shop, in a tiny kitchen, Lakhubhai himself would sit over the karahi frying jalebis, samosas and bhajis. Everything was of a high quality and people didn't mind paying for the product.

In 1962 neighbours in Kentish Town started complaining about the noise and the aromas from the Pathaks' busy kitchen and they were given three months' notice to find non-residential premises. Lakhubhai found a disused grain mill going for a song in the countryside, 70 miles from London, and the Pathaks shifted operations to Westbury. At this time they also dropped the 'h' from Pathak, to make it easier for westerners to pronounce and the famous brand name 'Patak's' was born.

Meanwhile the students who were Lakhubhai's faithful customers started asking him to stock pickles. Lakhubhai ordered a consignment of 20 kg but received 200 kg instead. That was the beginning of their pickle trade. Lakhubhai realised that the pickles were coming semi-blended and he had no control of the recipe. There was no continuity of flavour. He started modifying them and selling them under his label, which became immediately popular. The factory in Westbury started churning out pickles and chutneys, and supplies were driven to the London shops in two minivans loaded to the top.

Next, the students – who were continuously dictating the agenda – asked Lakhubhai if he could blend some spices so they could cook in their homes without the bother of having to stock ten spices. Lakhubhai got to work blending the spices in oil and after several tries the curry paste was born. 'He was servicing the demands of all his customers. The students would ask him what they wanted, and he would do it,' said Meena Pathak.

There were now enough funds for expansion and Lakhubhai bought another shop after a rice dealer went bankrupt owing him £13,000. The new shop in Westbourne Grove in West London was given to Kirit to look after. He was only sixteen at the time.

Kirit Pathak had watched his parents sit behind a hot stove for 18 hours a day. He had learnt how to make jalebis and pedas, and had done countless deliveries during his youth. But fresh back from boarding school in Ireland, complete with an Irish lilt in his voice, he now wanted to do higher studies. Kirit wanted to do business studies and his elder brother wanted to be an accountant. The two sisters joined the family business.

Lakhubhai Pathak found that he was losing hands; the sons wanted to study. 'What are you studying for?' he asked them. 'You are not making any money.' At this time Lakhubhai had done some bad business deals and the company was suddenly facing losses. Kirit Pathak was called in to help. Leaving his dreams of business studies, Kirit joined his father's business. It was the early seventies and he himself was barely eighteen. In the past, Kirit had helped his mother and packed spices. Now he decided that if he was going to take over, he was going to get to the grassroots of the business. He asked his father to go on a short holiday.

> Lakhubhai Pathak was a very dominant, very stubborn, very honest man, but he didn't have too many skills on the business side. He was more creative [said Meena Pathak]. When Kirit told him to go on holiday, he was very reluctant to leave the factory and business in the hands of an eighteen-year-old.

At this time Kirit's elder brother, Bharat, was managing the shop front in Drummond Street. His sister was looking after the imports and a second sister was doing the secretarial work. The youngest had not yet joined the trade. The uncle in Italy stepped in again and persuaded his brother to trust his son and go on holiday.

Lakhubhai and Shanta Gauri went to India and the kingdom was left in Kirit's hands. But young Kirit was to have a shaky start. As soon as Lakhubhai left the country, the entire sixteen-strong staff at Westbury went on strike. The staff were all white, had seen Kirit grow up over the years, and were not prepared to take orders from a kid. Besides Lakhubhai had been indulgent, and used to spend a lot of time chatting with his employees, but Kirit was immediately a more exacting boss.

Kirit took it calmly. He told the employees that they could go on strike if they wanted to, but they should also bring their resignations with them.

The staff panicked. Realising that the young lad was a tough one to crack they sent a message that they would all be at work the next day and they were sorry for what they had done. The next day the factory was running to full capacity. With Kirit at the helm, sales gradually turned around and Patak's was back on the map.

In 1973, Britain received from Uganda the first wave of Indian refugees expelled by the Idi Amin regime. As transit camps in Britain rehabilitated Indian refugees, the Pathaks capitalised on the new market, supplying the camps with proper Indian food. Business picked up as there was demand, and Kirit Pathak worked long and gruelling hours making deliveries and getting orders. 'The impetus was an ambition to get my mother out from behind the gathia karahi,' says Kirit Pathak, who had grown up seeing his mother sweating out all her life behind the hot stove.

Meanwhile, Lakhubhai, a man of restless energy, became involved with the film industry in India and wanted to produce a film. He eventually did and produced *Gayatri Mahima*, a religious film which flopped badly. But once in Bombay, Lakhubhai wanted to start up a production factory in the city, so he would have some control in India. Again the project was a failure and things deteriorated. Kirit now became virtually in charge of the business in London and came on frequent buying trips to India.

Bharat, the eldest son, married and was still in charge of the shop at Drummond Street. Kirit's mother was beginning to get frightened that her sons would marry white women, since there were no Indians in Westbury and they were being brought up in an entirely white environment. She now wanted to see Kirit married.

On one of his buying trips to India, Lakhubhai sent a proposal through a common friend to Meena, a young graduate in food technology from Sophia College, who was working at the time as front-house staff at the Oberoi Hotel in Bombay. Meena could not have come from a more different background. Her father was in the army, with a transferable job, and she had been brought up by her maternal grandmother in Bombay. Coming from a liberal upper-middle-class family, she had studied in Fort Convent at Colaba and spent her summer holidays with her parents or her aunt in Ahmedabad. Her father had taken early retirement when she was eleven years old and the family moved to Breach Candy in Bombay. She then went to Bombay International, an upmarket international school, and grew up in an urban cosmopolitan environment. In 1973 she completed her hotel management course and took a degree in catering and food technology. In 1975 she joined the Taj hotel group, starting in the front office and moving on to banqueting. She then took a position with the Oberoi group and it was while working here that she met Kirit.

Proposals had been flooding in for a while for Meena, but she was determined not to marry:

I was young, enjoying myself. I had done a stint of modelling. I didn't want to get married. To top it all, I had this impression of 'foreign' boys. I just felt they were 'fat slobs'. I just had this image of them as merchants, as lazy people with too much money. And I was most reluctant when I got this call in the morning after my night shift, that I had to meet somebody that day.

Having worked two shifts that day, Meena was in no mood to meet this suitor in the evening. 'I'm not going to say "Yes",' she told her aunt who had brought the proposal. They had a long drive to Vile Parle in the suburbs to meet the Pathak family, and so Meena continued to wear her Oberoi uniform, trying to look her worst so that she could put him off.

But when I saw Kirit, he looked worse than me, because he was recovering from flu [laughed Meena]. Well anyway, everyone eyed each other up, we chatted for a while and then somebody suggested we two should be left alone to talk. Kirit was a bit surprised to hear that because he thought Indian families would be very orthodox. I told him that I had trained in food technology, but I don't think he heard, because he didn't know it till quite a while after we were married. Anyway the first meeting was over, and we left.

The next day Meena's uncle called her and asked what she thought of the boy. Still uninterested, Meena replied, 'I think he's OK.'

Her uncle immediately took this as a 'yes' and before Meena had time to think, the news had got around that Meena 'liked the boy'. News reached Lakhubhai Pathak, who was absolutely delighted and immediately called Meena's mother and said they were coming tomorrow to see her again.

Lakhubhai had the premiere of his film that night and he invited Meena to come for the screening and join them for dinner later at the producers. Meena, still unaware that the Pathak family thought she had okayed the boy, agreed to the film premiere because she was interested in films and wanted to check out what Lakhubhai had produced. She still wasn't remotely interested in Kirit Pathak.

So Lakhubhai and Kirit came over to meet Meena again. Still not too happy with the meeting, Meena remained in her jeans and T-shirt and still did her best to put them off. 'I sat cross-legged on the sofa, and chatted casually,' remembers Meena. 'My mother was very disturbed with my behaviour and Dad (Lakhubhai) thought I was terribly modern.'

Meena went to the film, where she sat at the back with some cousins of Kirit's and never got to speak to him. Kirit meanwhile was becoming agitated that nothing was progressing and he hadn't even spoken to Meena alone. Finally some friends helped out and suggested they all go for a drive where they would leave Kirit and Meena alone and pick them up later. At the park in Matunga, Kirit proposed to Meena and told her he had made up his mind and would like to marry her. Meena had by then started to like what she saw and agreed. 'I thought any marriage will be a gamble. Might as well say yes!'

At dinner Kirit told his dad that Meena had accepted. Meena went home late and went to bed without waking up the family. Early next morning she was being woken by her mother saying, 'You didn't tell me you'd said yes.' She had learnt it from Lakhubhai Pathak, who had called early in the morning to congratulate her. Always a man in a hurry, Lakhubhai wanted to have an engagement ceremony the next day before Kirit returned to London. A small engagement ceremony followed and three months later Kirit came back to India and married Meena.

At that time Meena didn't know that the Pathaks were in the processed food business. She just knew they had a famous shop in London. And Kirit did not know that his wife was a trained food technologist. It was, of course, to prove a marriage of like minds and a partnership that was going to give the Patak's business enterprise its biggest boost.

It was a cold, bleak and wet day in November 1976 when Meena Pathak came to the small town of Westbury where the Pathak family lived. The sprawling bungalow set in acres of land in the bleak countryside with no other buildings around came as a shock to her.

Meena was from urban bustling Bombay, an upper-middle-class girl from a small family. She had arrived at the Pathaks' residence and had to live in a big joint family – and it felt strange to her. The Pathak household consisted of Lakhubhai and Shanta Gauri, Kirit's elder brother and wife, his sister and younger brother, and Kirit and Meena. Another brother lived with his wife in a separate house a mile away, but they had all their meals in the main house and were usually present there as well. Kirit's elder sister had married by then and lived in Madras. The fact that it was a working house meant that things were all over the place, and Meena was not used to an untidy house. Neither was she used to all the other aspects of living in the West: washing dishes, vacuuming the carpet, dusting, washing clothes, cooking and managing without servants. While the positive side was that the full house meant she wasn't lonely in a new country and had instant friends, the downside was the Hoover, the cleaning and the drudgery of housework.

My whole day seemed to go just doing household chores, washing and cleaning. I was so tired by the end of the day. For a long time I never knew what Kirit did, and I never even enquired what he did. Besides I didn't drive, so I'd get stuck at home while everybody else would simply drive off.

Uprooted from a privileged family background, Meena Pathak suddenly found herself in the thick of a working-class family, slaving in the kitchen and over chores. Though she was living in the

West, married to a successful business family, she began to miss her old life in Bombay, which had been far easier with servants and small luxuries. But fate had brought her to a virtual workhouse in London and it took her a while to adjust.

One day, Kirit noticed her looking tired and worn and asked her whether she would like to come with him to the factory. Meena immediately agreed. She was picked up and driven to the site by his brother. As Kirit was taking her proudly round the factory, Meena found herself asking a lot of questions. Kirit, who had never registered the fact that his wife was trained in the food business, asked her how she knew so much. When he found out, he had one solution for her: come to work. Meena accepted the job offer delightedly. She was now in charge of product development, and a new future for Patak's was about to be launched.

With her expertise in catering and food technology, Meena got to work. She had always felt that the Pathaks, because of their Kenyan background, did not know the real flavours of India. Meena started experimenting with tandooris and tikkas, the authentic popular Indian flavours. She started cooking different meals at home. Here again she found resistance in the kitchen. Shanta Gauri, doyenne of the Pathak kitchen, did not want to hand over the reins to her daughter-in-law. But Meena carried on nevertheless. Every day she cooked different flavours, she mixed and mashed and finally recreated a paste which could be put into a jar. A new spice mix was born – the tandoori paste – which revolutionised Indian food in Britain. It took Meena Pathak three months to develop the perfect tandoori paste.

In 1977 the Pathaks got their first major coverage in the British media. The *Daily Telegraph* newspaper, in an article on international cuisine, mentioned Patak's as being an authentic Indian company. At this time Patak's was still catering very much to the needs of the local Indian community and was not in the mainstream. Kirit had dabbled with exports, but the American market was not yet ready for Patak's. The post-parcel service was operating but business was stagnating.

The article made a major difference to the company. The next day the Pathaks got a call from food distributors Parish and Fenn who said they would like to distribute Patak's products. The Pathaks invited John Parish and John Fenn over for a meal. Meena laid out her tandoori paste, her kebab paste and a line-up of her other dishes. She was still only twenty-one at the time. One taste and the Pathaks were signed up. Parish and Fenn took up the distribution mandate and overnight the products were in 150 stores nationwide. Suddenly Patak's products were in multiples and had hit the high streets.

Production grew as demand grew. The whole family was now fully involved. Kirit's younger brother handled marketing, his elder brother did the accounting. The sisters married. The Pathaks outgrew their premises at Westbury and now wanted to introduce a canned product without adding oil. The plant in Westbury had no facilities for canning. The hunt for a plant began, and the family found one in Abram, Lancashire, where the damp moist north-western English climate was good for preserving spices. The plant was on four acres of land and had canning facilities.

In 1978, it was time for the Pathaks to move again. This time it was Kirit and Meena who made the move. Like his father and uncle before him, Kirit took Meena and their one-year-old son and left the family home at Westbury to move to the new site. It was as if history was repeating itself. The family packed their belongings and drove up to Wigan, where Kirit had rented a semi-detached house. Here it was a start from scratch. The factory was empty with only one production line. There were only three employees and Kirit and Meena Pathak worked all hours. Their little boy was looked after by a babysitter.

For a year they lived in rented accommodation, while the family in Westbury started winding down operations there. Over seven to eight months the Westbury site was closed down and the running of the Drummond Street shop was handed to Kirit's sister's husband. The rest of the Pathaks – Lakhubhai and Shanta Gauri, Kirit's elder brother, his wife and children and his younger brother – all moved up to Wigan. The Pathak family was in business again.

Meanwhile Meena Pathak, who had abandoned the Hoover and the washing machine, busied herself promoting Patak's at international exhibitions and building up media awareness of Indian cuisine. At a tasting session in the Asda supermarket in Edgeware in north London, in late 1983 or early 1984, she found the food was moving off the shelf as fast as she was supplying it to customers. The branch manager, having noticed the instant success, called up his head office immediately and overnight orders were placed by Asda supermarkets for Patak's products. Finally Patak's had hit the big time and were now out of the corner shops and into the main supermarkets.

This was the time when Indian food was seeing a heightened interest [said Meena Pathak]. Madhur Jaffrey's TV programmes were drawing mass audiences, television dramas like *Jewel in the Crown* were rekindling Raj nostalgia, and every little bit helped to promote Indian food in the mainstream.

Patak's now started manufacturing curry sauces, pastes, pickles and chutneys, which were snapped up from supermarket shelves.

In 1989 Lakhubhai Pathak decided to retire and divide up his empire between his sons. Kirit and Meena had been running the unit for some time now. They decided to buy out the other members of the family and become full owners of Patak's. Kirit's brothers left for the USA where they set up their own businesses. Lakhubhai and Shanta Gauri shuttled between Wigan and India.

Business prospered under Kirit and Meena. Under Meena's skilful guidance the company changed its image, going from pickles to pastes and from the local Indian community to the wider English market. No longer was Patak's a corner shop product: it was now on every supermarket shelf in Britain.

Slick bottling, labelling and packaging with handy recipes on the back made Patak's products stand out and compete with major brand names like Sharwood's and Uncle Ben's. Meena Pathak introduced sixty-nine varieties of Patak products (more than the famous Heinz range of fifty-seven) and modernised the company. A slick advertising campaign followed as Patak's ran full-page ads in the main British media and advertised on television. 'Pukka people pick a pot of Patak's' ran the campaign and the Pathaks soon had the English cooking chicken tikka masala instead of their Sunday roast.

In 1994 Patak's hit the headlines again. A survey by Mintel of the fastest growing brands in the UK showed Patak's to be the leaders in the market over multinationals like Coke and Calvin Klein. That a family-based outfit manufacturing pickles and pastes had taken on the multinational giants came as news that stunned the corporate world. The press coverage was endless. Huge colour spreads of Kirit and Meena Pathak sitting with their spices popped out of every British newspaper. The media focused on their rags-to-riches story and held them up as ideals of the immigrant success story in Britain. Patak's had well and truly arrived.

When Lakhubhai Pathak saw the media coverage, he had tears in his eyes. Largely illiterate still, he couldn't read the articles, but it stirred him to find that *he* was being written about.

For Mum and Dad, it was a matter of survival, a case of finding some way to feed the family [said Kirit Pathak]. They couldn't believe what their dream had achieved. They would have tears in their eyes when they walked down the production lines.

And the achievements were plenty: today Patak's is a household name in Britain. Whether you're shopping at your corner shop or a supermarket or at the exclusive Fortnum & Mason, you will find their jars and cans. If you are eating at a restaurant you are probably having food cooked in some Patak's sauce. Patak's exports to forty-five countries and has three production units in England. In 2000 it opened a new factory in Leigh, near Wigan, creating a hundred more jobs. It has twelve dedicated factories in India. Patak's supplies 92 per cent of Britain's Indian restaurants and has a turnover of £45 million. Over 15–20 tons of pickles and pastes are churned out from its factories every day, and then are packaged and loaded onto waiting trucks which take them across the country. Patak's have also entered the chilled and frozen food market and supply a range of

Indian dishes, naans and rotis to supermarkets. The new factory, built on principles of Feng Shui, even has a meditation room where Kirit himself sometimes leads sessions with staff.

Three-quarters of all Indian food sold in Australia comes from Patak's. The US market has seen an invasion of Patak's products after a joint venture with distributors Hormel. The product has been slightly modified for the American palate. Patak's has also entered into a partnership with Knorr to launch a separate line of products.

At her head office in Wigan, Meena Pathak says she hasn't lost her sense of perspective. As accountants tell her the latest sales figures on her way out, she smiles and worries about what meal she will cook at night for the three children and mother-in-law. 'Once I'm out of the office I'm no longer an executive,' she laughs. 'I'm a mum, a daughter-in-law, a wife. I still cook the meals myself every day, and look after the house.'

She drives a personalised Mercedes which says 'I WON' while Kirit drives one that says 'PTK 57', 1957 being the year that the Pathaks started their journey to fame. Jazzy cars, private schools for the children, a seven-bed mansion in Bolton and exotic family holidays are the only indulgences of the family, which has been regularly listed by the *Sunday Times* as one of the top 500 richest families in the UK.

But out of the home, Meena wears a different hat. She travels constantly, doing promotions for the company or educational trips to raise the profile of Indian food. Every two or three months she goes to India to keep up with the new recipes and trends and to discover more. Travelling to the interior and especially the coastal areas, Meena has been constantly modifying and introducing new flavours to the market. 'We are now entering an era of fusion cuisine when different things are being tried. I have to also educate people in the West that Indian food is not all hot – there is a tremendous variety in India,' she says. In October 2002, Meena Pathak published her first cook book, *Flavours of India*, a product of her extensive recipe-hunting and creation.

Her travels also take her on the hunt for the best spices and products from different parts of the world:

I can taste chilli powder raw and tell which region it comes from. The whole test is to get it constant, so that consumers know that what they get will taste the same and have the same high quality. Sometimes I have to work on endless combinations to get the product tasting just right and exactly the same. But nothing leaves the factory with a Patak's label unless it has been thoroughly vetted.

Recipes are kept as close secrets between Kirit and Meena Pathak. Only four other top people in the factory working in the blending rooms know them and are sworn to secrecy. When the spices are blended they are all done under code names. At the wet bottling plant where onion, garlic or tomato puree may be added to the pastes, the workers work on another code. No worker will know what went into the paste or powder at the other factory and the secret will be kept. Like the owners of Coca-Cola, who keep the original Coke formula in a vault in Atlanta, the Pathaks keep their recipes a close secret.

While Meena does her promotions, product development and recipe research, husband Kirit travels around the world hand-picking the best masala to be sent to the Lancashire factory.

The spices come from all over the world – mustard from Canada, garlic from Italy, mangoes, lime and ginger from Brazil or India, chillies from Peru, Pakistan or India, tamarind and coconut from Thailand, coriander from Iran, chick peas from Morocco, fenugreek from India – to name a few. The Pathaks are known to go into the field themselves and select the right seeds.

If for some reason the spices or herbs cannot be obtained from the same source, it will be Meena's job to modify them and blend them till they match the flavour, and taste the same as the previous batch. All recipe development is done at the head office in Wigan. 'We still import whole spices and actually grind them in our factories here, though it is more effort. But that is the way to ensure that it has the maximum flavour and freshness,' said Meena.

While Patak's papads are made in a dedicated factory at Madras, Patak's pickles are made at the

Lancashire factory. The raw mangoes are diced in India, salted, put in brine, and sent in huge barrels to Lancashire. Once here, they are then given the traditional Patak's recipe treatment. Because of the long time-span from locating the spices to importing and processing them, every recipe has to be planned at least ten weeks in advance.

The Pathaks import 500 tons of coriander powder a year, 350 tons of cumin, 250 tons of turmeric, 500 tons of chillies, 500 tons of mango pieces, and 400 tons of limes per year. Their four factories provide employment for about 500 people. The Wigan factory and the head office alone employ 250 staff. 'All our staff are white, and we have never had a problem with labour,' said Meena. 'They have been with us for years and are very loyal.'

The present Patak's range includes vegetable ready meals and daals, chutneys, cooking sauces in bottles and cooking sauces in cans, pickles, papads, soups, pastes in bottles, nans, rotis and breads, and the new range of ambient ready meals which require no refrigeration and may simply be heated and eaten.

The popular brands include the korma curry paste, the madras curry paste, the tikka masala cooking sauce, the rogan josh cooking sauce, the do-piaza cooking sauce, the jalfrezi cooking sauce and the balti cooking sauce. Patak's lime, mango, chilli and mixed pickles are served regularly in every Indian household or Indian restaurant in Britain.

So popular are the pastes and sauces that Meena Pathak said she has seen them selling in Bombay's Chor Bazaar. 'There is a demand in India for the sauces and pastes,' said Meena. 'I would love to set up a factory there. I think there is a market as people get busy and need to make quick meals. It is definitely one of our long term plans.'

But at the moment exports to forty-five countries and supplying the ever-increasing British market are keeping the Pathaks busy. Patak's has also entered the market for chilled ready meals and have started supplying supermarkets. The Patak's range of ready meals are stocked by Waitrose, Asda, Co-ops and other leading supermarkets.

The Pathak children – Neeraj (25), Nayan (23) and Anjali (21), all of whom are studying business management and marketing – are already being geared for the next decade of the Patak empire.

While Lakhubhai remained illiterate until his last days, though he could converse fluently in English, Hindi and Gujarati, and Kirit himself was forced to abandon higher studies and join his father at the age of seventeen, the third generation Pathaks, brought up in relative luxury, have had the privilege of the best education. They have also been trained by the best professional managers employed at the Patak's factory and have received hands-on experience in management skills. 'I'm sure they will benefit from these,' said Meena Pathak. 'They already have ideas, they are Pathak children and I'm sure they'll carry on the business well.'

But before ending the chapter with the third-generation Pathaks, we have to go back to the original crusader, Lakhubhai Pathak. Lakhubhai will be best remembered in India as the Non-Resident Indian (NRI) who took on the might of the Indian government and dragged former Indian Prime Minister P.V. Narasimha Rao to court. Lakhubhai issued a writ against Narasimha Rao and god-man Chandraswami for fraud claiming that in 1983 he had given $100,000 to Chandraswami, Rao's guru, on the understanding that Rao (then foreign minister) would secure Lakhubhai a government contract to supply paper pulp. The contract never materialised. Confined to a wheelchair, Lakhubhai made several trips to India to give evidence to the High Court in New Delhi. The case was dramatic as it was the first of its kind and Lakhubhai made headlines in the Indian media. Accompanied by wife Shanta Gauri, who stood by her temperamental and stubborn husband like a rock, the couple talked to reporters and frankly vowed to carry on the battle till the end. Rao himself was released on bail pending the outcome of the case. Sadly, Lakhubhai Pathak never saw the end of the case, as he died suddenly in April 1997 when the case was at its peak. Just five months earlier he had been giving spirited evidence in Delhi. He was seventy-two when he died and still gunning for Narasimha Rao.

The Pathak children, always a little embarrassed by Lakhubhai Pathak's public crusade against the

Indian Prime Minister, did not want to get involved. Throughout the case, the message from the Lancashire headquarters always was that it was nothing to do with the company and was purely a private affair.

The infamous case will be lost in the files of the Indian legal system, as none of the other Pathaks wants to take on the fight. Meena Pathak recalls how Chandraswami came to their house in Bolton when the deal was being done and how she mistrusted him immediately. It was pressure from her that stopped Lakhubhai paying more to Chandraswami.

> He was very angry with me for some time after that [said Meena] . . . But then he realised why I had said it. He became obsessed with the case and couldn't bear to be cheated. He himself was a very honest man.

At Lakhubhai's funeral in Manchester, the crowds came thronging. He was an icon for the immigrant Gujarati population. He had made it against all odds and was the ultimate success story. Wife Shanta Gauri wept in grief for the husband of fifty years who had taken her from Kenya to London and never let down the family. All the major British newspapers carried obituaries and everybody paid their respects to the man who had started an empire on £5.

Samosas, pickles, chutneys and pastes were how Lakhubhai started. Although he handed over the reins of his kingdom to Kirit and Meena in 1976, he had provided the solid base on which they could further their expertise, making it the first family of Indian processed foods in Britain today.

5

The Story of a Curry King

It was the winter of 1994. In the cold evening air, Gulam Khaderboy Noon was parking his car near Park Lane. His mobile phone rang as he was pulling up. The brief conversation was enough to make Noon hit the road again immediately. It was the news every manufacturer dreads to hear – a fire in his factory. The 40-minute drive back from the Dorchester Hotel – where Noon was due to attend a charity dinner – to Southall was one of the most anxious he had ever made.

When he reached the factory, it was engulfed in black smoke. The million pound state-of-the-art factory from where G.K. Noon churned out tons of chilled and frozen meals to supermarkets was covered in flames. Firemen were battling with the fire, but the hose-pipes seemed to have no effect at all. One hundred and fifty people had been working in the evening shift in the factory. A large crowd was standing silently in the orange glow of the fire watching the factory burn to cinders.

Noon's thoughts turned first to the staff. 'Is everybody out?' he shouted. They were. Quickly his family gathered round him. His daughter, brother and production manager were all there. 'Everyone is OK,' they assured him. 'We counted everybody as they came out. Nobody's injured.'

The firemen had a tough job beating the fire. No amount of water made a difference. It was far too dangerous to go in, so they concentrated on dousing the flames. Noon stood with his family, the 150 workers and other bystanders watching as his labour of love simply crashed down in flames. Several workers, who had been part of the factory from its launch, cried helplessly. Touched by their loyalty, Noon fought back his own tears. 'We'll build another factory, God willing,' said Noon. 'A better one, don't worry.'

All through the cold November night, the fire raged. It was not until about 3 a.m. that it was finally brought under control, although it was still smouldering. Several million pounds-worth of machinery and equipment were now a pile of acrid smelling molten metal and ash. Noon returned home shattered and exhausted. The workers left in gloom, glad they had survived, but worried about their future. Noon tried hard to fall asleep. Tomorrow would be another day.

Noon claims it was the relationship he had built with his staff and his suppliers that stood with him in his hour of crisis. He puts it down to the values he had inherited from his mother of respecting everybody and being a good employer. The phone never stopped ringing the next day. A long line of colleagues, friends, and workers all came to offer their sympathy and practical help.

One lady even offered Noon her entire savings of £72,000 for him to rebuild his factory. 'It was the sheer loyalty of my workers and colleagues that pulled me through,' says Noon. 'I refused to give my workers notice. I had 225 people working for me at the time. I knew we had to pull through.'

The first reassurance came from David Sainsbury, chairman of Sainsbury's, the super-market chain, to which Noon supplied chilled food. Sainsbury's offered to take most of Noon's staff and absorb them in his head depot at Hayes and Wembley until Noon was ready to start production again and re-employ them. Noon's reputation in the market was standing him in good stead:

With everybody standing by me, we came up with a solution in three weeks. We had two factories at Bombay Halwa. One of them could be used for the food process, we thought, and put the plan to our clients.

They agreed, and almost immediately the work began on converting the plant to a food factory. A month after the fire, production was restarted, initially at 40 per cent. In the meantime, Noon scoured round for another factory and found one in Wrexham in north Wales. The frozen food section began operating from Wrexham while the chilled food operated from the reconverted Bombay Halwa plant. Soon production went up to 90 per cent.

Extended credit was given, Noon's reputation ensured his clients' support, and once the insurance settlement was made, Noon found a factory site in the same area in Southall. The factory belonged to Metal Box and a quick sale and possession followed. By March 1995 the site belonged to Noon. 'The old Metal Box factory was stripped and rebuilt entirely,' said Noon. 'And on 13 August 1995 we opened the new site. It was less than a year since our old plant had been completely destroyed.'

Full production began at the gleaming new Noon factory on 22 September 1995. David Sainsbury inaugurated the factory in the presence of the Indian High Commissioner. The new factory was double the size of the old plant. Two carved brass elephants stood outside the doors, welcoming visitors to Noon Products plc. Inside, the walls were lined with paintings: Noon is a keen art collector, and has a range of Hussains. There were also paintings of Indian villages and markets. A special painting commissioned by Noon was one of the village of Bhawani Mandi, his ancestral home in Rajasthan. Painted by Delhi artist, Anu Naik, it shows a vegetable and spice market in the village and adorns the boardroom of Noon Products.

A new chapter had begun for Noon. Standing with the top names of the food retailing industry next to him, Noon was overcome with emotion and announced a week's bonus to his 300-strong cheering and supporting staff. It had been a dedicated journey for them, from the brink of unemployment and the dole to getting back on the scrubbed and gleaming factory floors of the new Noon Products plc in a record eight months. It was as much their day as Noon's.

The new factory stood on 55,000 sq ft and Noon had plans to build another on 45,000 square feet next to it. The empire was expanding. Noon had kept his word on that fateful November night. He had built another factory and it was bigger and better than the one before.

To Noon, the gleaming factory, risen out of the embers of the old, represented another dream come true in his adopted country. Even back in India, it was his dreams and vision that had kept the business expanding.

Born in Bombay in 1936, Noon was only eight years old when tragedy struck his family. His father died grieving for his eldest son, leaving the young family without a breadwinner. The double death left the family in shock. Noon's mother, had to cope with looking after the six children (three sons and three daughters), of whom Noon was the second. The family business was a confectionery shop started by Noon's grandfather in Bombay's Crawford market in 1898.

Noon's father was from Bhawani Mandi in Rajasthan but had moved to Bombay. His mother was from Iran. The shop begun by his grandfather – Royal Sweets – was doing well, but the untimely death of his father dealt a blow to the family. But like all Indian families, the joint family took over.

A cousin came to Bombay to take charge of the business and act as head of the family. The main thing was to keep the business going so Noon's mother and the children could be looked after.

Noon spent his days in school and his evenings in the shop. Everybody was expected to do their bit. Noon needed no pushing. While other kids of his age were playing cricket in the park, Noon would be learning business skills in the shop, or just helping to pack, unpack and deliver. Royal Sweets had a good reputation and business was brisk. In the mornings he would be up at 6 a.m. to take lessons from the family accountant. When the time came to leave school, Noon knew it was time for him to formally join the business. There was no other road for him to take and instinctively he wanted to improve the business and give it his best shot.

He was eighteen at the time, and India was still a newly independent country living in the euphoria of the Nehru years. Noon began to plan ahead. His sole ambition at that time was to improve the family situation and make sure his mother was financially secure. He also dreamt of possessing a car. With his first salary of 100 rupees, Noon bought himself a bicycle. He was getting there. The car was waiting for him and he knew it.

In 1962 he decided to modernise the shop premises. Always interested in technology, he installed air-conditioning in the shop, something considered a complete luxury in those days. He also redesigned the shop, spending a large sum of money on refitting, redecoration and buying top-quality furniture. His friends and advisers were horrified. It hardly seemed the sort of thing a small shop did. But Noon was determined and had a vision. He was going to grow. The shop started by his grandfather was going to be a household name in Bombay.

He proudly put up the new sign of Royal Sweets outside the shop. It worked. The newly designed, air-conditioned, gleaming shop attracted more customers than ever before. Noon was ready to move on. Royal Sweets was not going to have the gulab jamuns being fried on the premises. He now wanted a factory.

The head of the family was still the cousin. Noon had a spot of convincing to do and went on to acquire 5,000 sq ft for a separate factory for food preparation. Soon two more shops were bought. Royal Sweets was growing and in five years Noon had made it a household name.

Noon's primary concern was securing the future for his family. He bought the apartment block where Royal Sweets was situated and turned the place around. The building had been shabbily managed and there were about seventy apartments. Soon the building was spruced up, his mother and brothers were all lodged in comfortable apartments, the rent from the tenants assured a steady income and Noon could now discard his bicycle for a motorbike.

Noon now expanded into the paper industry and set up another company, Paper, Print and

Products. The business is now run by his brother in Bombay and is still a profitable one. The next diversification was a construction company, Bombay's biggest boomer, and the Noon coffers continued to grow. The cousin had stopped questioning Noon's initiatives now, and everyone had full confidence in him. Noon himself had fulfilled his initial dream: he now drove a small Fiat car.

As always he began to look for bigger fields to play. In 1964 he made his first trip to London. It was a difficult thing to do in those days with foreign exchange being very limited, but Noon arranged it anyway. Staying with a family friend in Southall he toyed with an idea: bringing tinned sweets to Britain. He even brought a few samples to show around. It would have been impossible for an Indian to come from Bombay at that stage and set up a business. But with the community network of Asians, Noon managed to get financial backers and soon it looked as though he could make the jump. In 1970 the idea came to fruition. Noon left Bombay to set up a branch of Royal Sweets in Southall. In 1973 production started in the first sweet shop and with that Royal Sweets had crossed the seas. 'I was a man at the right time at the right place,' says Noon modestly. 'Luck has a part to play in any business.'

In Noon's case it was the large influx of refugees from east Africa that fuelled demand for his sweets. The community settled largely in London and Leicester, and there was now a big demand for

Indian sweets and savouries. Business grew from the one shop outlet in Southall to seventeen outlets with branches in several cities. At present there are forty-two branches of Royal Sweets.

Again, Noon built a brand new factory. Technology was something he strongly believed in, and soon he had two factories producing sweets for Royal. Also quickly popular was the famous Bombay Mix, which proved an instant hit as a cocktail snack hitting pubs, restaurants and homes. Quality packaging was Noon's strong point. His famous rasmalais came vacuum-packed with special seals so as to retain their freshness. Noon had travelled as far as Norway to perfect the packaging. Having opened branches of Royal Sweets up and down the country, from London to Leicester and Bradford, all in areas with a heavy ethnic population, Noon looked around for more business.

In 1979 Noon decided to go further west – to the USA. In a joint partnership with the Taj Group of Hotels he moved to New York, where he set up a frozen-food factory providing chilled and frozen Indian food. But it didn't quite take off (Americans had not yet developed a taste for Indian food) and Noon soon sold his shares to Taj and went back to London. But in the meantime he had not wasted his time in the Big Apple. Noon did extensive research into the technology required for the bulk manufacture of Indian frozen food. 'I had a vision that one day Indian food would land on supermarket shelves with a vengeance,' said Noon.

'And that was what I wanted to concentrate on then.' He returned to Southall – often referred to as 'mini India' because of the large Indian community living there – determined to expand his confectionery business and assess the market for Indian ready meals. It was where Noon had started in the UK and it was where he would launch his future plans.

In 1988, in the peak Thatcher years when British business was booming and the future looked rosy, Noon founded Noon Products plc (now Noon Products Ltd). He established a factory for frozen and chilled Indian meals using sophisticated technology that would turn out more than a million meals a month without loss of authenticity or quality. Noon had entered the second phase of his business career, from confectionery to food.

His initial market survey was pretty basic: buying pre-cooked Indian meals from supermarkets and sampling them. Noon was not impressed. 'The quality was awful,' he said. 'They had no sense of what Indian food was like. There was chicken cooked with pineapple and sultanas and everything was churned together in a bland curry sauce.'

He decided to be upfront and think big. He didn't want to end up going to small shops and supplying them with Indian meals. Noon went for the biggest name in the frozen food business, Birds Eye. 'They were the biggest and best,' said Noon. 'It took a lot of persistence, I showed them samples and finally they were interested.'

At the specification of Birds Eye, the new factory was built on 6,500 square feet. The first order was worth £2.4 million. Noon Products had arrived. The whole family chipped in – working with the staff of eighty – to meet the target. By now Noon's daughter, Zarmin, a qualified food and beverage manager who had been working with the Taj Group in India, joined him. A management opening was created for his younger brother. Soon the demand was so great that the factory ran seven days a week churning out the Birds Eye range of Indian frozen meals.

Meanwhile British Airways also signed up with Noon, to get chilled meals for their Indian flights. Noon products were gradually gaining a position at the cutting edge of the market.

Next, Noon wanted to be on the supermarket shelves with chilled meals. It was 1989 and still the boom period in Britain. More and more working people and couples wanted to just pop into a supermarket, pick up a ready-cooked chilled meal and head home. Noon went to meet David Sainsbury. Asked what he thought about the Indian food on the shelves, Noon was forthright. 'It's not authentic,' he shot back at once. Sainsbury was shocked with the arrogant Indian, but took on Noon's offer to better the quality. The contract was signed which was to put Noon firmly on the rails in the Indian chilled food business. Today all Sainsbury's Indian chilled meals are cooked at Noon's Southall factory and eaten the length and breadth of the country. Supplying to one of the biggest food retailers in Britain was a clinching deal for Noon Products.

Once established, the contracts continued to grow. Waitrose, the food branch of John Lewis, wanted Noon products in 1989. Another super-market chain, Somerfield, also signed on. The Welcome Break group, Britain's premier motorway restaurant chain, also wanted an Indian menu as did several other retailers. Even France wanted a bite of Noon, and his factory won a contract to supply the Auchan chain of hypermarkets throughout France.

Noon's dream factories kept on growing to accommodate demand. They now occupied about 30,000 sq ft including five factory units and other units for cold storage, warehousing, laboratories and other facilities.

Then came 1994: the fire, disaster and recouping. Undaunted and determined, Noon's empire continued to grow. The next conquest was winning the contract to set up an Indian restaurant at Heathrow Terminal One. Heathrow was hallowed turf, the snack bars and restaurants were all Western. This was the first Indian restaurant to open in Heathrow. Significantly, it was not in Terminal Three, from where most of the flights to the subcontinent leave, but in Terminal One, which has major European and domestic flights. Noons, the restaurant, opened on 29 October 1996 and Noon had reason to feel pleased. What had started as a sweet shop in Southall was now a major player in Britain's mainstream food-retailing business.

The restaurant soon won the Egon Ronay Award for the Best Airport Restaurant.

But Noon soon realised that restaurants were not his forte and he pulled out of the restaurant business and began concentrating on further expansion. Noon Products Ltd started a product-testing laboratory and soon Noon Laboratory Service was launched, which would test food manufactured by other companies as well.

Britain recognised his achievements and awarded him an MBE in the 1996 honours list. The honour was presented to Noon by Prince Charles. Then came the final icing on the cake. Gulam Khaderboy Noon, who had started his business selling sweets, was knighted by the Queen in 2002 for his services to the food industry. From now on, he would be known as Sir Gulam. A modest Noon immediately insisted that his friends would only ever be allowed to call him simply 'G.K.' or 'Noon'.

Today Noon is exporting his ready-made meals to France, Germany, Switzerland, Spain, Belgium and Italy; has built a second factory on 45,000 sq ft near his new one; and opened a third factory in June 2003, built on an area of 108,000 sq ft.

Noon's factories now cover an area of over 200,000 sq ft, making the company the biggest Indian food manufacturer in Britain. Within its boundaries are situated the various plants like the chicken dicing plant, vegetable peeling plant and the cold storage plant, to name a few. The 30-m-long turbo tunnels and computerised conveyor belts, computer-controlled dual tilting bratt pans, huge marinaders, sauce kettles, programmable giant ovens and sensitive detecting and weighing equipment are a far cry from the karahis, ladles and cooking pots used in traditional Indian cooking. But it is the only way to get the same taste day after day in over a million dishes that leave the factory every month.

The figures are awesome: Noon Products churns out around 150,000 meals a day, seven days a week. Over a million meals are produced every month. His 850-strong workforce distributed between the various plants chops, dices, grinds, churns, stirs and packages the meals which finally leave the factory-floor in neat cartons ready to hit the supermarket shelves. The machines process about 200 tons of raw ingredients every week. Staff work 8-hour shifts, between 6 a.m. and 10 p.m. After the last shift is over, the night shift starts work, cleaning the plant and machinery and making sure they are clean and microbiologically safe for the next day's shift.

Noon's factory uses 35–40 tons of chicken and 35–40 tons of rice per week. Every day the amount of rice cooked is about three tons, over five tons of onions go into the various curries every day, as do four tons of tomatoes. Over a hundred dishes are made at Noon Products. When the new factory opens next to the present one, it will double the capacity to 300,000 meals a day. The British it seems simply can't get enough curry.

Noon's managers chase around the globe to procure their spices and raw materials. Chicken comes from France and Holland, tomatoes from

Italy, and spices and rice from India. Orders are placed with major spice importers in the UK such as TRS or Natco, which are approved by the supermarket chains. As Noon's business grows, the day isn't far away when Noon himself will be identifying and marketing the spices from India, thus acting as exporter and importer.

> The whole concept of Indian food in this country has changed [says Noon]. People now know the difference between authentic Indian food and the sort of tasteless stuff you got earlier. Our aim is authenticity first and we aim to serve cheap meals which are tasty, healthy and safe. Our labs are of the highest standards and we monitor safety all the time.

Noon's biggest seller is the chicken tikka makhanwala, a variation of the ever-popular chicken tikka masala. His production director Ashok Kaul prepares the recipes and liaises with customers. An ex-Taj Group chef, Kaul's job is constantly to try new recipes, keep in touch with customer demand, and introduce new and varied flavours in the market. Kaul had come to Britain in 1975 as the chef responsible for the meals aboard Air India flights. Kaul enjoyed a high reputation and when Noon opened his first plant in 1988 he poached Kaul from Air India. Air India's loss was Noon's gain, as Kaul was quick to take on the challenge of bulk production and is constantly introducing new recipes to the Noon range.

Noon's daughters, Zeenat Harnal and Zarmin Sekhon, are also involved full-time in the company, as is Noon's younger brother, Akbar.

The hub of the company is the development kitchen on the mezzanine floor, where new recipes are tried every day. It is here – thankfully, with more traditional karais and cooking pots – that Ashok Kaul, his chief deputy Sainath Rao and a group of chefs (mostly headhunted from India's Taj Group or other top hotels like Windsor Manor, Bangalore) work on new recipes. If the customer requests a special dish like chicken jalfrezi, the Noon team will hunt out the authentic recipes for it. The best recipe will be worked out by cooking small portions several times in different ways and vetting it with the tasting panel. If the customer requests a new range of Goan dishes, then the team will have to organise between ten and twelve new dishes and go through the same process of cooking and tasting. Noon himself says he will never sell anything that he doesn't enjoy eating himself and takes a keen interest in the new recipes coming out of the development kitchen.

Once the tasters have decided on the dish, the recipe is fed into the computer. Instead of the small portion that was cooked in the development kitchen, the computer works out the proportions for bulk cooking for as much as 400 kg of chicken or lamb.

The rest is left to the machines on Noon's high-tech factory floor. No pots and pans here, as the vast amounts of food are cooked by machines, which grind the masala, churn the curry and even pressure-cook the lamb. The only difference is that the spices are introduced into the meal separately, as is done in authentic Indian cooking. A worker on the factory floor will be throwing bay leaves or curry leaves when needed into the giant machine. Even the chopped dhania leaves are added later, as is done in Indian cooking.

Ashok Kaul says he realised that his use of whole spices in cooking had caused a few surprises in the British market when he got some letters from customers complaining that they had found wood bark in their meals. It was, of course, a piece of cinnamon. The letters were duly replied to and Noon and Kaul feel that the use of whole spices has enriched the cooking and at the same time also educated the customer.

Dishes cooked with whole cumin seeds (jeera) have often surprised the customer when he has bitten into it and released the strong flavour. We like our customers to taste the individual spices and don't believe in grinding them up and putting them all in together [says Kaul].

Hygiene is top priority and all the kitchen workers are in special sanitised uniforms. Visitors are not allowed in the factory for fear of infection. They can see the proceedings on video or have to wear the special clothing.

The food is tested for salmonella and listeria at several stages of cooking and even the workers are tested so that there are no carriers. Noon's laboratory has acquired a formidable reputation and the group now provides the Noon Laboratory Service, which is accredited by the Food Research Association and tests food made by other manufacturers.

Meanwhile, after the cooking and food safety checks, it is time for the packaging and sealing. Most chilled meals are cooked the day before and packaged the next day, ready to leave the factory by evening. But there is one more stage between the cooking and packing. It is the all-important tasting. After the food is cooked, another round of tasting takes place at the development kitchen before the food is loaded on to the waiting Noon trucks and begins its journey to the supermarket. 'Ours is a chef-oriented factory,' says Noon, 'which is why I always appoint top chefs from India for my product kitchen.' The latest range of Noon products has gone heavily into regional Indian cuisine with dishes from Bengal, Maharashtra, Andhra Pradesh and Tamil Nadu.

Apart from supplying the supermarkets with their chilled and frozen meals, Noon introduced his own brand of frozen meals which is stocked separately by retailers. The 'Noon' meals range is available in Harrods, Europa, 7-Eleven, Harts the Grocer, Shepherds, Partridges and other leading supermarkets in the UK. Noon's own brand range includes dishes like traditional chicken curry with rice, chicken tikka makhanwalla with rice, thai red curry and coconut rice, prawn masala with rice, chicken tikka pasanda with rice and tarka daal. All the dishes have proved popular.

Noon has introduced some Indian sweets from Royal Halwa on supermarket shelves. Though Royal Halwa has traditionally catered to the Indian market (the British have not yet developed a taste for *gulabjamun* and *rasgulla*), some supermarkets had shown interest in keeping small portions of Indian sweets along with the Indian chilled meals as an accompaniment. The supermarket choices are *rasmalai* and *gajar ka halwa*, both sweets which need not be too sugary and can probably be enjoyed by the British palate. Today the sweets are available in little dessert packs in Waitrose.

Noon has reason to be pleased with his achievements. There was a time he dreamt of owning a car. Now his personalised number plate says N1 GKN. He has been knighted, been declared the Asian of The Year (1994), and is a familiar face in both London's Asian cocktail circuit and in his native Bombay. With a turnover of £80 million, Noon has constantly featured high on the list of top 200 Asian millionaires published by *Eastern Eye* and the *Sunday Times* with an estimated fortune of around £47 million.

He has been closely involved with the Prince's Trust, which brings him in close contact with Prince Charles whenever the latter organises a charity dinner for the Trust. In March 2001 he presented a cheque for £215,000 to the Prince's Trust, which helps Asian businesses. A framed letter from Prince Charles in Noon's central

London office at Queen Anne's Gate thanks Noon for his work with the Trust and for the enjoyable evening at the Dorchester and the gift of the carpet which now adorns the Prince's residence in Highgrove.

There is also a letter from Prime Minister Tony Blair thanking Noon for his work with the Tower Hamlets College, where he is involved with mentoring. Recently, Noon became the focus of media attention for donating £100,000 to the Labour Party, with the media linking it to his knighthood and a cash for favours controversy. 'Why would I want to give it *after* the knighthood,' an exasperated Noon told the media. 'I have always been a Labour Party donor.'

Apart from charities in Britain, Noon continues to retain strong links with India where his brother is running the family business. He has charitable interests in Rajasthan, his ancestral home state, and continues to support two hospitals built by his family in the 1930s. He has also built three schools in Bhawani Mandi. In 1969 he was appointed a Justice of the Peace in Bombay. In early 1998 he surprised the expatriate Indian community in Britain by writing a letter to *India Today* magazine saying the BJP was the best party to govern India and deserved to be given a chance. The letter caused some ripples because Noon is a Muslim and comes from Bombay which has seen considerable communal tension in the recent past. But it is an indication that Noon keeps closely in touch with India and probably sees future growth there.

When some letters of Mahatma Gandhi were being auctioned at Sothebys in London in July 1998, Noon responded immediately to a request by the former High Commissioner to London, Dr L.M. Singhvi, to help the Indian government bid for the letters. The letters were duly procured for a whopping £20,700 and Noon, along with another Indian businessman, Nat Puri, gifted the letters to India. 'It was a chance to do something for India, and we were proud to do it,' said Noon.

Noon's golden moment came when the Queen knighted him at Buckingham Palace on 10 December 2002. The Queen did the honours and exchanged a few pleasantries with him. She asked him what he did and remarked that Indian food was doing very well in Britain. Noon reminded her that he had earlier in the year sat at her table for a Golden Jubilee celebratory lunch at Gunnersbury House.

She has a fine sense of humour [said Noon]. When the girl who was serving dropped an ice bucket just near the Queen, I apologised on her behalf, and she immediately said: 'Oh don't worry, we do it all the time at home.'

Accompanied by his wife, the film-maker and writer Mohini Kent (whom he had married in 1998 after his divorce from his first wife came through), the couple walked out of the palace feeling – quite understandably – that the world was their curry.

When not busy planning philanthropic activities, more curry crusades, or attending black-tie dos and socialising, Noon's next interest is cricket. He is an active member of the Gymkhana Club in Osterley in West London and is on a committee to modernise and expand facilities at the club, which has entertained the Indian cricket team as its guests and at friendly matches.

With one eye on the curry market and one eye on cricket, Noon regretfully said he would not be travelling to South Africa for the World Cup cricket match in 2003. The reason: his younger brother had won the toss! He himself would have to watch India v. England on the television. Even curry kings can't win all the time!

6

From Muzaffarpur to the Midlands

On driving through the high-security gates at the
S&A factory at Derby, one is immediately
enveloped in the unmistakable smell of Indian
food. Inside, a row of chiller trucks stands ready,
being loaded with the ready meals that make their
way to supermarkets and hotel chains. This 5,000
sq m factory space is the empire of Perween Warsi,
owner of S&A foods, the busiest businesswoman
in the Midlands, and high on the list of Britain's
top 100 entrepreneurs. For the petite, perfectly
turned-out Warsi, the £80 million empire of S&A
foods is a long way from the place of her birth in
Bihar, one of India's most backward states.

Born in 1956 in Muzaffarpur, Perween Jaffrey
was the second of five children. Her father was a
civil engineer who travelled around Bihar on
assignments with his three sons and two
daughters. Perween's childhood was spent in
different towns and cities as the family was
transferred every two years. The constant moving
meant Perween had to learn to make new friends

all the time and she still feels it is a quality that has helped her in life.

It was a full and happy childhood. Little Perween was often looked after by her mother and grandmother and there were always plenty of friends. One thing she remembers is her own little kitchen set, which was a favourite with her. Even at the age of two, she loved playing cooking games. Her grandmother would often give her some vegetables and flour to play with and Perween would be quite absorbed with her rolling pin, making dough for chapattis. She always wanted to contribute to the busy family kitchen.

The family travelled to Ranchi, Purnea, Patna and several other towns and districts in Bihar. In 1971 when her father was posted to Ranchi, her marriage was arranged to Talib Warsi, a medical student. His family was also from Muzaffarpur and his grandfather was known to the Jaffrey family.

Being from a conservative Muslim family, Perween placed her full faith in her parents and agreed to marry Talib without meeting him or even seeing his photograph. 'I knew they would choose the best for me, and I had complete faith in my parents,' says Perween. 'And they did.' She was only fifteen at the time.

But she recalls that, even though she had consented to an arranged marriage, she still had a lot of dreams. She wanted to open a school which would provide not just education but love and care and would not treat its students harshly. She wanted to be a progressive teacher who could look after slow learners. But destiny had other things in store for Perween. She was not going to be a school teacher in Bihar, although she didn't know that when she married Talib Warsi.

Talib Warsi was then in his final year of MBBS at the Prince of Wales Medical College in Patna, and within weeks the marriage was arranged. Talib finished his medical exams, received his internship, and the Warsis set up their first marital home in Patna.

In 1973, their first son was born. And in August 1974, Dr Talib Warsi decided to go to the UK to do further studies. In 1975 Perween Warsi followed her husband out of Bihar and into the UK for the first time. 'I didn't know much about England then, everybody thought we would go back. But I somehow knew we would stay,' said Perween. 'The only thing I knew about England was its famous weather.'

It was the month of January when Perween Warsi first set foot on British soil. The sun was shining gorgeously when she stepped outside the plane, contrary to everything she'd always been told about grey and damp English winters. 'The sun has followed me since,' she says happily. 'I have had the most wonderful time in this country.'

Life abroad began for the Warsis in the pretty north Welsh town of Rhyll where Dr Warsi worked in the local hospital. It was a quiet town, unlike anything the Warsis had ever been used to. 'Everything was different,' said Perween, 'the weather, culture, food, language, the people, but I quite enjoyed it.' Perween loved the beach, and found the people very helpful and friendly. Living near the hospital, they had a lot of doctors for neighbours and never felt lonely. Soon Perween was busy entertaining and hosting parties and inevitably doing a lot of cooking. She found the housework hard, not being used to cleaning and washing dishes, but everything was a new experience and soon she was settling in well. Son Sadiq was two and a half years old now, and life was already quite busy.

Dr Warsi next moved to a hospital in Dewsbury. It was here while he was on duty at the gynaecological wing, that Perween gave birth to her second son, Abid. At that time, Perween wanted to remain a housewife, giving her full attention to her sons. She always wanted to have a career some day, but it wasn't on the immediate agenda.

Britain still needed getting used to and the English way of life was growing slowly on the couple. One day Perween saw the 'SOLD' sign outside her neighbour's house and immediately asked her with full Indian curiosity how much she had sold it for. Her neighbour told her she must never ask such questions. So Perween asked why not. Her neighbour explained to her it was not the culture in this country to ask such personal questions. Perween knew then that the English were truly different and that her Indian frankness and inquisitiveness would have to be controlled here. 'I was still so innocent then,' she laughs now. 'I had a lot to learn. But the differences always made life more interesting.' She was still very inquisitive however and wanted to learn as much about the country and its people as possible.

In 1979, Dr Talib Warsi set up a practice in Derby in the Midlands. Life went on in very much the same way: there were always people over and the Warsis did a lot of entertaining. One day Dr Warsi invited some English colleagues for dinner and Perween cooked a complete Indian meal. She recalls how reluctant everyone was to try the meal. The impression they had was that curry was hot, and the wives were telling their husbands to take the first plunge. But once they plucked up the courage to begin, Perween soon found that very quickly they were all tucking in and really enjoying themselves. Her dinner was a hit.

There were always people over for meals and once her friends told her to take it up professionally, Perween started toying with the idea. By the mid-eighties Indian food was already becoming popular in the market and Perween felt that people should have good quality Indian food that was not bland and tasteless. She started thinking of supplying good quality authentic Indian food. 'I thought of the supermarkets straightaway,' said Perween Warsi. 'I could have opened a takeaway or a restaurant, but that was not what I wanted. I wanted my food to be distributed through the network of supermarkets all over Britain.'

Perween began by making some finger foods – she made half a dozen samosas and took them to her local takeaway to see if they would sell. 'Thinking back now, I can see that I was unconsciously doing market research, to see if anyone wanted the product,' said Perween. 'It was important for me to know what people thought about it. In commercial terms it could be seen as testing the market.' So the samosas went on the food counter at Andy's Fish Bar, a bar that still exists in Derby. The owner was Greek, and soon he was on the line to Perween telling her that the samosas had gone very quickly. Perween was on to her first order. Soon she was supplying Andy's Fish Bar regularly and other orders from other takeaways began to flow in. Perween was busy, she was happy, but she was not satisfied. She still had her eyes on a national chain.

Before long she needed to recruit a few women to give her a helping hand. Perween went to recruit a local Indian housewife in Derby. She still can't forget the experience. The housewife was a Punjabi lady who was excited but nervous. She was keen to earn some extra money but apprehensive about going to somebody's house to work. Finally she said she would go to Perween's house if she could take a friend with her. So Perween ended up with two helping ladies instead of one. The ladies were wonderful, said Perween. They worked uncomplainingly for long hours, chopping, cooking and cleaning. The kitchen was now functioning for about twelve hours. The volume grew to meet extra demand and Perween suddenly found that her kitchen was too tiny to take the load. Next to the kitchen was the conservatory, where her husband kept all his plants.

One fine day, as the samosas demanded more space, Perween packed her husband's plants into the garage and simply took over his conservatory. She remembers how upset he was when he returned home from work and found that his plants had been unceremoniously removed from the conservatory and a line of pots and pans had moved in instead. 'In retrospect, he can think it was an investment that paid off well,' she laughs. 'Because by now business was in full flow.'

The Warsi boys, Sadiq and Abid, were in the meantime going to the nearby Repton School at Derby, which was a boarding school. So Perween had plenty of time. Her old dream of having a career was still very much on her mind. Her kitchen had extended into the conservatory and she had five ladies working under her. 'I was always focused,' said Perween. 'We were busy and working hard, but I always remembered my goal, and that was the national chain.' Sticking to her target, she repeatedly rang the supermarkets. But the only response she received was to be asked to send her price list and product list. That was not Perween's style. She wanted to sell her products face to face, making her buyers taste them.

Finally one day, she rang Asda supermarket and said: 'I've tried your dishes and they are bland and boring.' She could feel the silence at the other end of the line. But it worked. Soon she got a call from Asda. They were reviewing their Indian food products and were having a blind tasting. The year was 1986. Perween Warsi packed her products and sent them to Leeds for the blind tasting. She was pretty confident but nervous. The next day she got a call saying her products were through.

> I was so excited. I had waited for months for this, and it had finally happened [said Perween]. But though I was so excited, I knew that it was important for me to have a long-term relationship with them and that demanded complete honesty, trust and openness on my side.

Perween desperately wanted the business and could see her dream finally being fulfilled. But in her meeting with Asda top brass, she was completely honest and upfront. When they told her they had selected her products and would be placing bulk orders, she told them honestly that she did not have a factory and was working from her kitchen. 'There was shock and surprise on their faces,' said Perween. 'There was silence for a while and they all looked at each other. And then they told me to set up a factory.' It was the big moment in Perween's life but she had to act quickly. Perween and her husband went scouting for a factory. They found a car valeting garage on 200,000–300,000 sq ft in an industrial unit and rented it. Overnight the factory was cleaned, painted, partially tiled and fitted with sinks.

Then, knowing that she had no experience of these things, Perween decided to invite a director of a local laboratory to give his view. Perween thought she had done a fairly good job on the decorations, and was horrified when the expert said her factory would never be cleared. 'What's wrong?' she cried in horror. She had thought the new sink and the painted green wall looked good enough. 'It's no good,' he said matter-of-factly. He told her the whole place had to be redone. It had to be fully tiled, it needed steel tables, sinks and a lot more work. What was worse was that the Asda inspectors were coming within the next 28 hours to look at her factory.

But Perween was not one to be put off easily. She was determined to do it if it meant staying up the full 28 hours to do so. A patient of her husband's was in the tiling business. But he had booked a holiday and was going to leave the next day. She begged him to come to her rescue.

People were very kind to me [said Perween]. He actually cancelled his holiday, he knew how much it meant to me, he brought five people and overnight the whole place was tiled and ready. We stayed up all night making coffee for the workers and keeping them going. I was determined to get this order and there was no way I was going to disappoint my customers.

The next morning she called in the laboratory expert to have a look again. He was absolutely stunned at the transformation and couldn't believe it was the same place. By the time the Asda team arrived the tables were laid out, the new sinks were gleaming, even the coat and hat racks were in place. Her friends came round as well for the final once-over and everyone was impressed. Perween says that it was exactly that sort of determination to succeed that had always characterised her work. 'Stay and finish the job' was always her motto.

Soon the factory production line was running and Perween's initial line-up was five finger items including samosas, bhajis and tandoori chicken. She recruited twelve people and within six months the volume was increasing. The factory was open 24 hours, with the workers coming in three shifts. Perween herself used to get up at 2 a.m. and begin work.

As the factory workers were all women, coming in and going out at odd hours, Perween preferred to pick them up herself and bring them to the factory, as their safety was her prime concern. She would drop the shift that had finished and bring in the fresh shift for the night. One night, as she was driving twelve women to the factory at 2 a.m., she was stopped by a policeman, she says:

It was something I had always expected would happen. It was quite natural for the police to wonder where a woman was going in the middle of the night with a carload of women. Anyway, one day the police did stop us. They knocked on my car window and asked what I was up to. I explained that I was escorting the ladies to the factory. And they let us go. It was quite an amusing experience.

Perween always gives a lot of credit to the women who worked long hours with her at the factory. Many of them are still with her. The orders kept pouring in and soon Perween had to purchase the unit next door and expand her factory. The necessary chillers and ovens were fitted and the business rolled on.

One day as the ladies in the factory were completing their 12-hour shift and packing to go home, the phone rang. It was Asda asking for a larger production order. Perween says she felt quite sorry for the ladies who worked virtually seven days a week, and didn't feel like asking them to stay longer, but they had heard her talking on the phone and told her they would meet the order. 'That is how closely we have worked,' said Perween. 'We have always worked like a family. And the ladies simply stayed on and finished off the order. It is also our philosophy, that we never short our customers.'

As the orders grew, Perween's staff increased to forty. There were now a few Chinese boys and a few local English boys being employed as well. By 1987 orders were coming in from Safeway and Asda and Perween felt that they were already outgrowing the factory premises. Soon another unit next door became available and they quickly leased it, knocked down the connecting door and made it one large unit double the size of the old.

By now the trend was towards pre-packed meals and Perween was keen to get ahead on that front. But the company needed funds to get into chilled meals. Investment soon came her way in the form of Hughes Food Group which led Perween on her next stage of expansion.

The factory was built on 20,000 sq ft in 1989, producing ready-to-eat meals on an industrial site in Derby. The very first week the factory churned out 5,000 meals. The company was named S&A after Perween's two sons Sadiq and Abid. Demand grew rapidly and soon it was time to expand further.

But there were slight hiccups despite the success. The Hughes Group went into receivership, taking their shares in S&A with it. There was great interest from potential buyers to buy up S&A. But Perween was not going to let the empire she had built up slip away so easily. Together with her husband they had a management buyout and after a tough battle and with support from the 3i venture capital group they bought back the business and regained control in November 1991.

Once in total control, there was no stopping the Warsis who grew from strength to strength. In 1996 they opened an additional £8 million factory on the same site to meet the increased demand. Today the two plants at the Sir Francis Ley Industrial Estate churn out a million meals a week, supplying Asda, Safeway, Co-op and Budgens supermarkets and also hotel and leisure chains like Whitbread, Scottish and Newcastle, and Granada.

The business today has a turnover of £80 million and employs 1,000 people. Perween Warsi is one of the biggest employers in the region. A second factory in Newcastle-under-Lyme was started in 2002 which employs another 1,000 people and aims to employ 1,200 people by 2004. Perween launched her own brand of products in 2001 calling it 'Perween'. At her factories, staff jokingly call her 'Chief Spice'.

Perween had been singled out for praise by Prime Minister Tony Blair at a function for Asian businessmen in 1997. Now it was her time to be honoured by the Queen. Having already received the MBE in 1997, Perween was honoured with a CBE in 2002 and went to Buckingham Palace to receive her award.

Perween's curries are exported to five super-markets in France as Indian food begins to become popular on the continent. Her products are also sold in supermarkets in Holland and Belgium. She has now extended her food range to include Chinese, Thai, South American, Mediterranean, north African and other exotic world foods. Under her own brand name, Perween, she launched a Tapas range with three varieties: spicy meat, vegetarian and a seafood selection. The tapas dishes are served in a terracotta-style dish and have become very popular.

Perween believes in being ahead of the game. 'One of the secrets of our success has been to anticipate consumer demand and create new products and ranges to fill that demand well in advance rather than following somebody else,' she says.

For her Indian selection, Perween headhunted chefs from five-star hotels in India. When she launched her range of Chinese meals, she collaborated with world renowned chef Ken Hom. Here again, Perween felt she had to get her Chinese cuisine to be authentic and spent a whole year persuading Ken Hom to work with her. A Chinese chef was also recruited in-house. The same pattern of authentic recipes was used for the world food range.

Always keen on the complete product and with a sharp eye for design, Perween designed a giant wok and even won an award for it. The world's largest wok installed in the factory can cook on high heat just like a proper wok. It was part of her constant attention to detail and innovation.

Her offices in Derby have turmeric-coloured walls to recreate the colour of the spices that are being used in the factory. One of her prized possessions is her trophy cupboard full of all the gleaming cups and crystals that she has won. These include being listed among the top 100 entrepreneurs in Britain (ranked twenty-first) for 1998, being elected Woman Entrepreneur of the World in 1996 in a function in Los Angeles, beating off entries from all over the world, a British Quality Food and Drink Award in 1994, winning the Veuve Clicquot Businesswoman of the

Year 1994, Midlands Businesswoman of the Year also in 1994, the Food Manufacture Award in 1994, the 3i Award for Manufacturers in 1995, RADAR People of the Year Award 1995, *Sunday Telegraph* Food and Drink Award 1995, besides others. The University of Derby gave her an honorary degree in 1997. The MBE and CBE followed, all of which makes her very proud. 'I find business a lot of fun. I haven't found being a woman a disadvantage,' said Perween. Her parents, who live in Patna, can hardly believe their eyes when they see her now: a confident businesswoman running an £80 million empire. 'Given my background – my family was a very orthodox Muslim family – it's probably incredible,' admits Perween. As for her keen business sense, she thinks she's a natural. Nobody in her family is in business – her father was an engineer, her brothers are professionals, even her husband is a doctor:

> I think I saw there was a niche in the market, and I stepped in. A lot of successful business also has to do with being in the right place at the right time. And we were prepared to work very hard and never compromise our standards.

Dr Talib Warsi is now involved full-time in the company as marketing director, but he still continues to run his surgery.

Not surprisingly Perween has become a role model for young Asian girls in Britain and can often be seen giving talks at universities or appearing on television programmes. It was no surprise that Tony Blair picked out Perween Warsi and S&A Foods as an example of how British Asians had done well in business starting from humble beginnings. Perween Warsi was the perfect example. From making samosas in her kitchen she had single-handedly created an £80 million food empire and taken her place among Britain's top entrepreneurs. Not surprisingly she has earned herself the name of Curry Queen.

Perween believes in being fully involved with her business from concept to delivery. Recipes are planned in the development kitchen and fed into computers. Meanwhile the packaging is designed and the finished product leaves the factory only after rigorous checks. She also believes in creating new ideas at every stage. Apart from the award-winning giant wok, she also created the concept of packaging a ready-to-eat thali meal, containing two vegetables and a meat dish and being a complete meal in itself, and supplying it to supermarkets.

In 1997 S&A celebrated its tenth anniversary and featured the ten longest-serving staff from the earliest days. All 600 employees were invited to the party, which was attended by the former President of the Department of Trade and Industry, Margaret Beckett. It was also the day S&A won a contract from British Airways to supply in-flight curries.

Perween values S&A as a family-run business and likes to think of the whole organisation as a family:

Our oldest workers have been with us from the beginning. They worked tirelessly 12 hours a day and never said 'no' if they had to put in more time. They treated the business as a family business. And that's the way I like to keep it. Now we have grown so much, it is difficult for me to be personally in touch with all my staff, but I still organise meetings when I sit and talk to them and handle any problems that we may be facing.

The workers at S&A are not unionised, and Perween prefers it this way. She says when the unions had approached her workers to join up, they had actually brought their union forms and handed them back to her. 'That shows the amount of trust they have in us. We work as a team, as part of a family,' said Perween.

In February 1998 S&A foods also had its first royal visitor as Princess Anne took a tour of the factory. The Princess Royal unveiled a portrait of herself, which hangs in the main corridor of the factory.

For Perween, success has come after a great deal of hard work and determination. From 1986, when she took over her husband's conservatory, to the ten-year celebration in 1997, the S&A growth chart reflects her focused plans for expansion and national distribution:

We are constantly innovating. After all, shopping should be fun and not a chore. The supermarket is becoming a destination where a range of services are on offer, rather than a shop where you simply push your trolley out of the door as soon as possible.

Perween's formula for success is simple. She firmly believes that authentic meals demand the right ingredients and the correct method of cooking. As well as achieving the taste, products must also look attractive and inviting. This again requires top-of-the-range production and processing equipment and the right people.

Consequently Perween has headhunted experts from all over the world who understand different cuisines. She has specialist Indian, Chinese, Malaysian, Thai and European chefs. One Christmas in 1995 Perween made a trip to India to bag a chef to bring back to Derby. She discovered Pratap Chinna at Oberoi Grand in Calcutta and Ravi Bajaj at the Taj Hotel in Bombay, who had worked under celebrated chef Satish Arora. Perween offered them the chance to work for her in Derby and they joined her highly motivated development team. Others on the team include Roxana Rashid (known as Rocky) and Jeaby Dale, the kitchen assistant who was a chef in a Thai restaurant.

The core development team is the heart of the factory, being involved in every stage of the production, from concept and creation to quality control. Perween believes in reinvesting in the business and is constantly buying the latest equipment to suit the production process. Some of this is even specially designed by herself for the specific process – as in the case of the giant wok.

The process from development kitchen to supermarket curries is not easy. It is important to carry out extensive trials with all new products, making sure the quality and taste are maintained from the development kitchen right through to bulk production. Even before the recipe is born, it is planned in the development kitchen and then executed as a sample. The taste panels then swing into action. These consist of a cross-section of staff from the factory, including quality assurance, personnel, chefs and supervisors.

Then follows extensive market research by conducting blind tastings. The recipe is finally approved when they have the support of the research behind them and the knowledge that the customer will be fully satisfied.

Once the recipe has been approved, there is a full-time trainer working in the development kitchen who understands the recipe and knows what is required from the customer's point of view. The recipe is then fed into computers for bulk manufacture and the factory floor takes over.

Perween herself is still enthusiastic about trying new recipes and loves nothing better than to potter in the kitchen, churning out a new dish. What she enjoys most about cooking is that she can see the complete product within minutes and judge the impact it has immediately. Collecting recipes and going in search of new ones is a constant obsession with her and she travels to India regularly in search of new and exciting recipes.

When not busy in her development kitchen or attending a board meeting, she likes to spend time with her family and friends. She enjoys working out at the gym and spends any spare time reading and listening to Indian music. Sons Sadiq and Abid are likely to join the family business one day. Sadiq studied law at university and Abid studied psychology, a subject that has always fascinated Perween. Both have shown interest in the business and Perween would like them to become involved – at their own pace.

Apart from supermarkets and hotels, Perween is also designing new menus for a new corporate hospitality and banqueting business, merging the best of eastern and western cuisine with an emphasis on quality and presentation.

The 46-year-old single-handed builder of the multi-million food empire says she can never forget her roots and her humble beginnings. She still goes back to her native town of Patna where her parents live and where she says she prefers not to get involved with any of the turbulent politics. Perween would love to do business in India but as yet has no plans. For the moment India still means relaxing holidays and the constant search for new recipes.

Back in Derby, she drives her personalised Daimler with the number plate SAF (for S&A Foods), which she says 'drives like the wind', and lives in the mansion that is the Warsi home. 'I think my husband has been very supportive in everything I have done,' says Perween. 'I could not have done it without him. And my friends have been good to me as well.'

Talib Warsi, referred to by the staff simply as 'the doctor', is an active part of the S&A team now. The two figure regularly on the list of the 200 richest Asians in the UK. For Perween there is still a whole world waiting to be conquered, but she never lets herself forget where she came from and who she is. 'The greatest thing is to be a good person, have your friends around you, and know that you are still the same person even though you now figure among the richest and most successful people in the country,' she says. And she should know.

7

Ruling the Restaurants

It was in the early 1920s that Edward Palmer, an Englishman whose family had been in India for four generations, came to London to study medicine. Palmer was the great-grandson of an English general and an Indian princess and he left behind him a sunny country, a host of servants and retainers and a cuisine to die for. London, in contrast, after the First World War, was a cold, bleak place.

Palmer was homesick and he missed Indian food. So in 1926 he set up an Indian restaurant in London. Located on Regent Street, Veeraswamy is still London's oldest surviving Indian restaurant. Veeraswamy's clientele reads like a veritable *Who's Who*. It soon became the stopping point of all the eminent people of India – maharajas, politicians, artists – when they came to London.

The legend ran that they would spend the first day resting and hit Veeraswamy the next. The food was a mixture, partly English and partly Indian. The menu consisted of exotic foods like rabbit, game and beef curry.

It was authentic Indian food prepared by Indian chefs. The restaurant overlooking Regent Street was extremely elegant and fairly expensive. There weren't too many restaurants in London at that time, and eating out was something still fairly unknown although there were clubs which served meals. Unlike the French, who had a culture of eating out almost a hundred years before the English, London had not exploded gastronomically. In 1926 Edward Palmer bought the whole building at 101 Regent Street and the restaurant became the centre for the rich, famous and fashionable and those connected with India.

Through the doors of Veeraswamy walked Edward, Prince of Wales, King Gustav of Sweden, Pandit Nehru, Indira Gandhi and Charlie Chaplin. In 1945 the restaurant included a daily weather forecast and a special theatre service, providing a complete list of West End plays. In 1959 Veeraswamy started serving tandoori chicken and became the first Indian restaurant to have a tandoor in Britain. Menus in 1959 offered the customer a choice between Indian, Pakistani and Ceylonese dishes. It also had a selection of English and French dishes.

The opening of Veeraswamy caused a buzz on the restaurant scene. Previously, Indian eating establishments had been opened for the use of Indians themselves and acted as community gathering places rather than commercial operations. It was in 1773 at the Coffee House in Haymarket that curry first appeared on a London menu. In 1810, the first establishment regularly serving Indian food, the Hindostanee Coffee House, opened in London's Portman Square. It was started by an Indian, Deen Muhammad, who advertised his restaurant as catering to 'Indian gentlemen'. The restaurant had hookahs for the use of its clients. However, the restaurant didn't last very long and Deen Muhammad moved to Brighton, where he set up a successful shampoo/massage parlour. The first Indian restaurant recorded by *Foodservice Intelligence Ltd*, an industry publication, was the Salut e Hind in Holborn in 1911, slightly preceded by the first Chinese restaurant, Maxim's, in 1908. Another very popular one was Shafi's, opened by Mohammed Wayseen and Mohammed Rayhim in London in 1920. But these were mainly for Indians although a few adventurous Europeans did dine there. But Veeraswamy put an elegant Indian restaurant on the West End map. Soaked in the Raj flavour, it was the place for the rich and famous of the Empire to take in London life. The Veeraswamy – with its authentic Indian chefs – became the training ground for thousands of staff over the years.

Next in line was the opening of the Kohinoor in London by Bir Bahadur and that led to his brothers joining him to open Taj Mahals in Brighton, Oxford and Northampton and Kohinoors in Cambridge and Manchester, all pre-1939. By 1950 the numbers were not much more than double figures, although the first of the many Birmingham restaurants to open (the Darjeeling, 1945) had already started trading.

In 1946 there were only three Indian restaurants in London: Shafi's in Gerrard Street, Veeraswamy and the Kohinoor. There were a mere six such establishments in the whole of the UK in 1948.

In 1960 there were still only around 500 restaurants, but immigration and the introduction of the tandoori clay oven in the mid-sixties led to a rapid growth to 1,200 by 1970. Restaurants like the Gaylord in Mayfair (a branch of the Gaylord restaurant in Delhi) became popular for their tandoori dishes in the late sixties and attracted a star clientele, including Ravi Shankar and George Harrison.

By 1980 the number had more than doubled again to almost 3,000. Today it has reached the 8,500 mark, with London itself boasting over 2,000 Indian restaurants.

In the fifties and early sixties, most of the restaurants were owned by Indians and Pakistanis and served north Indian fare, like rich kormas and biriyanis. After a long period of postwar austerity, the new restaurants became more popular with Britons identifying with the Raj decor and names, the friendly service and the cheap prices. By now the Bangladeshis had also entered the Indian restaurant business, putting their skills as cooks to the test.

It was necessity that prompted the newly immigrant Bangladeshis from Sylhet to start up their restaurants. Many had been crew members on the P&O ferries that came from India and had learnt different styles of cooking from other crew members. They learnt to cook Anglo-Indian dishes like Mulligatawny soup, Persian soup, and several

Lakhubhai Pathak (right) stands proudly behind the counter of his first shop at 134 Drummond Street.

Kirit and Meena Pathak with Patak's products.

G.K. Noon with Prince Charles and the former Indian High
Commissioner L.M. Singhvi.

Spices being sorted at
Noon's factory in Southall.

Spice queen
Perween Warsi
at her office in
Derby.

Karan Bilimoria brings Cobra beer to Harrods.

Afzal Butt near the sweet counter at Imran's restaurant in Birmingham.

Mohammed Arif outside Adil, one of Birmingham's oldest Balti restaurants.

Parminder Bains (Pele) in the kitchen of his Balti pub . . .

. . . and serving his enthusiastic customers.

The new-look
Veeraswamy restaurant
refurbished in 1997.

Michelin star chef
Vineet Bhatia of Zaika
restaurant.

La Porte des Indes,
London's only
restaurant serving the
food of the French
colonies in India.

The recently refurbished Red Fort restaurant, a Labour Party favourite.

Michelin star chef Alfred Prasad of Tamarind restaurant.

The upmarket Cinnamon Club housed in the Old Westminster Library.

Basmati rice being sold at a cash and carry shop in Ealing Road in west London.

Indian meals/products line the shelves at Sainsbury's.

The popular Indian selection at Marks & Spencer.

south Indian and north Indian dishes. Lack of other jobs in London at the time made them resort to taking on a profession that would become their trademark in Britain. The first flush of Bangladeshi-run restaurants in the 1950s all served what became known as the 'P&O' menu, which is different from the tandoori menus that most curry houses today have to offer.

Again purely for survival, the Bangladeshis soon started to take over from the Punjabi cooks and to cook the unfamiliar recipes of north India, giving them their own unique touch. This led to the birth of the famous one-curry sauce with which most Bangladeshi restaurateurs cooked all their dishes, and still do today. In most Bangladeshi restaurants, a korma meant a mild dish, a madras a hotter one and the mother of them all was the vindaloo, guaranteed to set you on fire. The intricacies of Indian cooking, the array of non-spicy dishes simply did not feature at the time.

To the English, the spicy Indian curry was the ideal accompaniment to pints of lager, and soon, taking on a vindaloo and several pints was the usual initiation to manhood for most British males. Sadly and unwittingly the curry house became part of a British yob culture as well.

It was, however, no yob, but King Gustav of Sweden who started the tradition of drinking beer with his curry. King Gustav, a great lover of Indian food, was a regular at Veeraswamy when he was in London and would have nothing but his Carlsberg beer with his duck vindaloo. These he would have imported from Europe and kept ready for him when he dined at Veeraswamy. Before Christmas he was known to ship a keg of Carlsberg to London.

The tradition of serving Carlsberg with Indian food was something that caught on in the Indian restaurants. Today the standard curry house serves Carlsberg as well as a range of Indian beers and Carlsberg is the most popular beer with Indian curries.

Over the seventies the curry houses continued to boom, helped by increasing immigration of Bangladeshis, and also of Gujaratis from Kenya and Uganda. The curry house had already become a standard affair with flock wallpaper, laminated menus and friendly service. The space was there for an upmarket fashionable Indian restaurant which would serve authentic Indian food to a discerning clientele. The market was further fuelled in the early eighties with television serials like *Jewel in the Crown* – still today one of British television's most highly-rated serials – which created a wave of Raj nostalgia. This was followed by films like *Heat and Dust* and *Gandhi*, all of which sparked off a craving for the subcontinent in Britain.

On 10 December 1982, the Bombay Brasserie was born on the site of the old and run-down Bailey's Hotel, close to Gloucester Road underground station. The brainchild of Camellia Panjabi, then Executive Director of the Taj group, the Bombay Brasserie was conceptualised as a place in London that would serve the cuisine of Bombay in an atmosphere of neo-colonial ambience.

It was a clear break from the run-of-the-mill curry house. By this time the previously fashionable Veeraswamy had declined in standard and the service and menu was tired. The only other reasonably upmarket restaurant was Shezan, opposite Harrods. The time was right for a new upmarket restaurant. Under the watchful eyes of Camellia Panjabi and Adi Modi, the general manager who was brought in from the Taj group's Sheba Hotel in Yemen, Bailey's Hotel was given a total re-fit. The large airy breakfast room of the hotel became the main dining area. Cane peacock chairs were brought in from Assam to furnish the cocktail bar. The original Victorian plasterwork was restored and touched up in pink, gold and eggshell blue. On the walls were hung paintings and prints of Parsi life in Bombay. Large ceiling fans were installed to recreate the Indian ambience and potted plants, exotic palms, and ferns all completed the colonial club atmosphere.

From March 1981 Camellia moved to London to oversee the restaurant to the last detail. 'I was quite clear what I wanted, a nice casual Raj atmosphere,' said Camellia. 'It was going to be something like Far Pavilions, a romantic view of the Raj in India as seen by people who had never been to India.'

Camellia also wanted to start something new in Indian restaurants: she wanted to plate the dishes and serve each dish with accompaniments. In most Indian restaurants people did not order individual dishes but shared from a large number of dishes. But Indian food would need a lot of accompaniments, so Camellia had to find big plates. The Bombay Brasserie is still famous for its big plates some two decades on.

When the big plates ordered from Belgium eventually arrived, the wine glasses looked too small. So the appropriate glasses were found and ordered in New York. Next Camellia went to Paris to look for dessert glasses, sorbet glasses and candle holders and simply carried them all back herself. Finally the photographs were framed, the artefacts from Bombay's Chor Bazar were put up and the Bombay Brasserie was ready to go. It opened without advertising as a 90-seater restaurant. It served 38 covers the first evening. All the takings went to charity. Camellia said she obtained photographs of restaurant critic Fay Maschler and put them up in the kitchen, showing them to all the staff. 'On the third day I returned to Bombay and as luck would have it, on the fourth day Fay Maschler walked in,' laughed Camellia. 'She was looking totally different and the staff did not recognise her.'

But Maschler had enjoyed the dining experience and her review next day was very favourable. The famed and feared food critic wrote in the *Evening Standard*:

The Bombay Brasserie brought with it a sweep of grandeur and an intelligible interpretation of the regionality of Indian cooking and at a stroke altered the pre-conceptions of a cuisine that had long been immured in yards of flock wallpaper and all-purpose sauces.

After the first set of reviews had appeared in the British press, the restaurant served 94 covers and was full to capacity. Within a year a conservatory was added, doubling the capacity to 175 and creating a special ambience that made it an immensely popular dining experience. A further extension to the conservatory was carried out in 1998 taking the seating to 265, and the restaurant is still full every evening.

The most popular feature of the Bombay Brasserie quickly became its crescent-shaped conservatory, which is routinely used for launches, functions, regular dining and even fashion shoots. The Bombay Brasserie became the first Indian restaurant to be mentioned in the same league as London's top eating places such as Langan's Brasserie (owned by Michael Caine), the Dorchester Grill and Harvey's.

The Bombay Brasserie has always boasted a top clientele and on any night you could be sitting next to Michael Caine, Sir Anthony Hopkins, Tom Cruise, Tom Hanks or Goldie Hawn, to name a few Hollywood regulars. The cricketing season brings in the likes of Sir Gary Sobers, Imran Khan and Ian Botham, while the Wimbledon fortnight has brought in Jimmy Connors, John McEnroe and Martina Navratilova. Royals who have eaten there include the Prince of Wales and Prince and Princess Michael of Kent. On one night in 1988, gossip columnist Nigel Dempster reported spotting Bruce Springsteen, Charlton Heston, Telly Savalas, Ali McGraw and Barbara Dickson all tucking into their curries at the Bombay Brasserie.

The Bombay Brasserie had the unique distinction of being the only Indian restaurant frequently visited by rock stars. Mick Jagger hired the conservatory to celebrate former wife Jerry Hall's thirty-fifth birthday. London's rockers and shakers Viscount Linley, Susannah Constantine, Pink Floyd's Dave Gilmour, Imran Khan and others were among the party-goers who rocked the night away to the strains of a raucous Cajun band. David Bowie and Iman also favoured the Bombay Brasserie, as did Paul and Linda McCartney. George Harrison ordered from the Brasserie for three of his parties at his country estate. Once Stevie Wonder, while dining there with television star Terry Wogan, took over the piano after dinner and treated the delighted guests to an impromptu concert. Sir Anthony Hopkins, who used to live down the road from the Bombay Brasserie, treated it as his local, often dropping in there for both lunch and dinner. For his sixtieth birthday he hired the whole restaurant on New Year's Eve. The party went on from eight in the evening to four in the morning and was a great hit. 'All the parties that have been thrown here by rock stars, actors and famous people have been huge successes, because we provide excellent food in an excellent atmosphere,' says Modi.

Hollywood stars have even taken away Bombay Brasserie food on their shoots. Tom Cruise once ordered food for his whole crew which was rushed into the waiting cab and taken straight to Heathrow, from where the Hollywood superstar carried his chicken tikka masala, chicken xacutti and lachcha parathas with him to Italy. Robin Williams is another Hollywood hero who has ordered meals to be delivered from the Bombay Brasserie. It is no surprise to see the Bentleys, Rolls-Royces and Jaguars lining up outside the Bombay Brasserie as celebrities drop off to dine.

The reclusive author, Sir V.S. Naipaul, had his wedding reception at Bombay Brasserie, entertaining a small and select number of guests at a dinner party. Composer Lord Andrew Lloyd Webber held his (second) wedding reception at the restaurant. And when *Vanity Fair* had a party to honour fifty years of Lord Snowdon's photographs of show people, they had it at the Bombay Brasserie. The evening was a glamorous one with numerous showbiz personalities in attendance.

Even London's top chefs can be seen dining at the Bombay Brasserie on their days off. Anton Mossiman, Nico Landenis and Raymond Blanc are some of the chefs who regularly visit the restaurant, often swapping notes with the Brasserie's executive chef.

Ask Adi Modi the reason behind the success story of the Bombay Brasserie and he'll tell you it is down to the authentic food, the service, and the ambience:

We changed the concept of Indian food in this country. We were the first to serve authentic Indian food prepared by a team of nine highly trained chefs, all from the Taj group.

Before I started this place I visited six Indian restaurants in London trying out the menu. They all tasted the same, and they were not Indian food by any standard. Bombay Brasserie became the first to serve regional Indian cuisine from Goa and the cuisine of the Parsis. All the other restaurants simply copied us after that.

One of Modi's full-time jobs was keeping track of the copycat Bombay Brasseries that continuously popped up all over the country and even in the USA. At one time there were seventeen Bombay Brasseries all over the UK. Modi succeeded in closing down eleven and sent legal notices to six others. There was even one in Texas and Modi had to get the legal machinery running again to close it down. Having poor copycats passing off as chains can be damaging, he says, and it is a serious business keeping track of offenders. Modi has now moved on as general manager to the Bombay Brasserie's sister restaurant, Quilon, which serves Kerala cuisine.

All Bombay Brasserie's chefs are chosen from the Taj group and they have brought about a wide regional Indian menu with a famous Sunday buffet that is changed regularly. Sixty-five per cent of the restaurant's clientele are local Londoners who come as many as three times a week.

In 1997 the Bombay Brasserie celebrated its fifteenth anniversary with a black-tie dinner for all its regular customers, and served forty dishes on the occasion. In 1998 it rebuilt a new conservatory and extended the seating from 175 to 265. The new conservatory – double the size of the old one – features a pond at the centre and a fountain spouting from a sculpted lion's mouth. The illuminated hanging baskets, the palms and banana trees, all recreate an ambience that gives the Bombay Brasserie its special touch.

Over the years the restaurant has won Pat Chapman's *Good Curry Restaurant Guide* Award for Best Indian Restaurant, and the highly respected *Real Curry Restaurant Guide* award for Best in Britain. It has won the Front of House Trophy from *The Real Curry Restaurant Guide* and the Best Restaurant Ambience Award from the *Good Curry Guide*.

Taking their cue from the success of the Bombay Brasserie, a spate of elegant upmarket restaurants started opening up in London over the eighties. These would use authentic Indian chefs, take care over the cooking and try to get away from the beer-and-curry syndrome that characterised most Indian restaurants. The Red Fort, in the heart of Soho, started by Bangladeshi restaurateur Amin Ali, threw out the flock wallpaper, brought in professional chefs and waiters and introduced a complementary wine list.

The Red Fort soon won lavish reviews and awards, and the celebrity clientele started dropping in to taste authentic Indian food in the heart of London's buzzing theatre district. Situated in a listed building in Dean Street, virtually swamped by restaurants on all sides, the mild-mannered Amin Ali worked round the clock to make sure the Red Fort maintained a high standard of culinary excellence and service. He recruited Naresh Matta, former senior lecturer from the Delhi College of Catering, and served up a menu which he described as 'the Food of Kings'. It was the quest for serving Mughal cuisine that took Amin Ali to India again and again and he recruited top Indian chef Manjit Singh Gill to join as a consultant.

Dishes like Shah Jehan's Lamb Stew became hot Red Fort favourites and the whole menu struck a balance between classical, regional and eclectic dishes. Ali also organised frequent food festivals to keep up the buzz of Indian food and to introduce new flavours to the English palate.

Ali's celebrity clientele included pop stars like Tina Turner and the Spice Girls, film and theatre personalities like Mel Gibson, Bruce Willis, Richard Attenborough, Emma Thompson, Jane Seymour and Ben Elton, to name but a few. Politicians, especially Labour politicians, were regulars at the Red Fort. A staunch Labour Party supporter, Ali has entertained Neil and Glenys Kinnock, Tony and Cherie Blair, all of whom are personal friends, and many prominent members of government. Neil Kinnock describes it as his favourite Soho restaurant and on one occasion, at a party in the Red Fort of the left-wing fashionable set, entertained everyone with a selection of limericks. There is even a Red Fort Parliamentary Privilege Club, with 1,000 MPs and peers as members. Ali, who has used his restaurant to hold several charity launches and been very active in the community, was even offered a peerage by Tony Blair, but declined. 'I am a restaurateur. I am not interested in politics. I support the Labour Party and I have many personal friends in politics. But this is my line and this is what I love doing,' he said modestly.

The Condé Nast restaurant guide singled out the Red Fort to dub it 'The Mother of all Indian Restaurants'. In 2000 the Red Fort had to close down after a fire but re-opened in 2001 after a £1.5 million refit with a brand new look and menu. The new Red Fort, with its red sandstone and marble imported from Jaipur, water feature and elegant decor, was immediately praised by the critics. Chef Mohammed Rais, formerly of the famous Dum Pukht restaurant at the Maurya Sheraton, Delhi, claims descent from a family of chefs who cooked for the Nawabs of Awadh, and has many family recipes tucked away with him. Some of these he has introduced at the Red Fort.

A spate of restaurants in the eighties, such as the Viceroy of India and the Star of India, all helped in promoting the market for Indian cuisine. The food was reasonably good, the prices slightly higher than average, and they set the middle route between top restaurants like the Bombay Brasserie and the high-street curry house. What was impressive was their profusion. By the end of the eighties there were over 5,000 Indian restaurants in the country.

The year 1990 saw the launch of a new-style Indian restaurant. Taking its cue from the Bombay Brasserie's neo-colonial appeal, London's second ground-breaking restaurant was the creation of Namita Panjabi, sister of Camellia Panjabi.

Chutney Mary caused a buzz the moment it opened its doors in fashionable Chelsea. The name itself, an Anglo-Indian term to describe a saucy westernised woman in the Raj days, was attractive enough. Chutney Mary came to London bringing with it Anglo-Indian cuisine, served in colonial surroundings and with the back-up of an excellent team of chefs making every effort to turn out the authentic flavours of India.

Eight years after the opening of the Bombay Brasserie, this was the restaurant that created a buzz in fashionable circles. Like the Bombay Brasserie, it had a conservatory, but the rest of the ambience was completely different. Chutney Mary delved into Raj nostalgia with a vengeance. From a menu that stirred up all the old memories of the Raj, like the delightful chicken dish, country captain, to salmon kedgeree and hill station bread and butter pudding, to the carefully chosen paintings on the wall reminiscent of the Raj, the presentation was complete. Old colonials, Chelsea groupies, India lovers, all trooped in through the doors of Chutney Mary, putting a smile on the face of Namita Panjabi and husband and co-owner Ranjit Mathrani.

Chutney Mary's speciality was also that it explored regional Indian cuisine, bringing the coastal dishes of India for the first time to the Indian restaurant menus. Malabari chicken, green Goan chicken curry, slow-roasted lamb shank became instant favourites and fired off a whole new rage in regional cooking. The Bombay Brasserie had always served Goan food, which remains hugely popular as British tourists who eat it in Goa come back asking for it, but Chutney Mary took coastal cuisine even further.

The awards flowed in, the Michelin Bib Gourmand Award for good food at moderate prices, the Curry Club Award for Best Indian Restaurant in Britain, and a mention by Fay Maschler as one of her top twenty favourite restaurants.

Chutney Mary has now moved away from serving Anglo-Indian cuisine to doing regional Indian cuisine, for which it has seven regional chefs from India. The restaurant was given a total revamp in 2002 and both the menu and decor changed to bring it in line with the twenty-first century. Namita Panjabi, a keen cook herself, takes a personal interest in the menu and is always looking out for new recipes that she can pick up from leading gourmet families in India, from Maharajah's palaces and humble wayside stalls. A special stone-grinder, imported from India, makes sure Chutney Mary offers its dishes with freshly ground spices, prepared every day. Today Chutney Mary offers such regional cuisine as Cochin-style squid fried with red chilli masala and herbs, crab claws with pepper and garlic, tandoori partridge and Mangalore prawns.

With the Indian restaurant surviving the recession of the early nineties, the takers simply kept on growing. As Indian restaurateurs realised the market was becoming saturated they started going away from the formula curry houses. From the mid-nineties a spate of elegant, modern, almost European-style Indian restaurants started to open in London and other British cities. In Birmingham there was the Shimla Pinks, Bradford had the Aagrah, in Edinburgh it was the Verandah, in Coventry, Country Joes, and in Milton Keynes, the Jaipur.

These were consciously aiming at the fashionable, trendy end of the market, desperate to get away from the stigma attached to the curry-and-lager digs. Restaurants became bigger, trendier, modern and vibrant, bringing a whole new image of Indian cuisine to Britain. Under the guidance of the dynamic Indian chef Cyrus Todiwala came the Café Spice Namaste in 1995, bringing a style of decor to an Indian restaurant that had not existed before.

Todiwala, head chef and owner, not only threw out the flock wallpaper, he nearly threw out the chicken tikka masala from his menu. Nor did he want the cool, elegant, upmarket, colonial elegance that the Bombay Brasserie and Chutney Mary had brought. Todiwala wanted to celebrate the colours of India: the colours of spices and silks. Saffron, sage, cinnamon, casbah blue, purple and fuschia became his colour scheme and the restaurant exploded with the vibrant colours. It was the colourful banners, and the exotic hues at his restaurant in Tower Bridge, in the heart of London's financial world, that caught the attention of critics from day one. The decor was described as Mediterranean, with its rich hues, stylish drapes, cane chairs, and the waiters in colourful Indian uniforms.

But to Cyrus Todiwala it was the colours of India, the buzz of an Eastern bazaar. Except this haven was located in an 1855 Grade II listed building that was a former court house and later a government office in a rather shabby inner street in the heart of the City, minutes from Tower Bridge. Not only was the decor innovative and exciting, Todiwala backed it up with a menu that made most Indian jaws drop. Out of Todiwala's kitchen came such exotic specialities as venison assado, duck pasandas, goose tikka cafreal, even lobster, bison and kangaroo.

Todiwala, a Parsi from Bombay, who spent a long stint as head chef and later executive chef at the Taj Holiday Village in Goa and the Fort Aguada Beach Resort, has an exciting range of Goan and Portugese cuisine at his restaurant. His speciality menu included Bolinhas Pescadore (Goan-style fish-cake), Prosciutto Carne De Javali (Italian wild

boar served with tangy garlic, basil and olive oil),
buffalo xacutti, assado de carne de veado (rolled
shoulder of venison cooked with onion, garlic and
red chillies) and even an emu abafado (emu
cooked in classical Goan masala with red chillies,
pepper, coconut etc.). His exotic menu included
food from the hunting families of Madhya Pradesh
and Rajasthan: guinea fowl pasanda, bhuna bater
mussalum, tar kaia (venison preparation for the
hunt from Mewar), and khade masaley ka pashula
bong (shank of venison cooked in the classical
style of the Maharanas of Rajputana).

The regular menu served dishes like kozhi varta
kari, chicken Tamil-style with cloves, cardamom
and tamarind paste, Parsee roast lamb (masala nu
roast gos), dhansak (with a fierce warning not to
compare it with dhansak served elsewhere – 'we
are Parsis and we know what we are doing'),
vindalho de porco (pork vindaloo), and beef
xacutti. There was also sword fish tikka,
Mangalorean chicken curry, vegetable sambar with
lemon rice and even an avial. Todiwala believed in
catering to all tastes, except that of the curry-house
uninformed.

Because of the exotic nature of the meats on
offer, Todiwala did a weekly speciality menu apart
from the regular menu, and these were served
simply until they ran out.

Our food is different from the menu offered by
any other Indian restaurant, not because of the
exotic meats, but because you can pick and

choose from the regions. To those who tell me that my menu is not Indian, I say it is. The preparation is Indian, though the meat may be a kangaroo. Besides in India they did eat venison, bison, wild boar. The largest bison is an Indian bison, the *gaur* or *nilgai*. Indians even eat alligators. I prepare alligator meat. My mother's family lived near Udaipur in Naseerabad, and had close relations with the maharanas. They used to eat kesar and gulab. A lot of my cooking influences are from that region. I serve peacock. It is a Muslim delicacy.

Todiwala makes his own venison, wild boar and bison pickles, which he sells at the restaurant. He says he is a keen environmentalist and will not serve any meat that is from an endangered species. He gets his ostrich from France, and his emu and kangaroo from Australia, where the latter is officially culled.

I believe in constantly experimenting with food. I tried crocodile meat tikkas, but it didn't work. Then I found alligator tasted better. I can't stay with one thing for long. I must evolve in my cooking. The strangest looking fish come through my doors, weird shellfish, which I am trying to learn to cook, I serve all sorts of exotic meats. But I serve it Indian style, that's the difference. And I have shown that these were eaten in India. Also I would never serve a meat that I could not eat myself.

Todiwala said he could not understand the Indian food that was served in this country when he first came here in 1991. The formula curries made him so unhappy that he didn't know how he was going to work in a restaurant here. So he took a gamble in the first restaurant that he worked for, Namaste, and changed the menu. Gradually it caught on, and soon Cyrus Todiwala was able to start his own restaurant with his own special flavours. 'I am serving traditional Indian food, but I am experimenting with different meats,' said Todiwala. 'People here don't know the sheer range of Indian food. I am giving them that.'

Most of the clientele at the Café Spice Namaste is white, although there are a few Indians working in the City who drop by with friends. It is when the Indians give the seal of approval that Todiwala feels satisfied. Although as chef-owner Todiwala has to abandon full-time cooking, he employs three chefs from Goa, one from Darjeeling and two from Pakistan, and some from Bangladesh. He still cooks the speciality menus and closely supervises the kitchen. 'I get my buzz from cooking, I cook every day. If not trying meals, I'm trying chutneys, jams, baking soda bread. I don't like to stop.'

Todiwala has won the Best Indian Chef Award several times, and Café Spice Namaste has won the Award for the Best Indian Restaurant Menu in Britain from the *Real Curry Restaurant Guide*, and the Best Indian Restaurant in Britain from the Patak's group. It was also a finalist in the *Time Out* Best Newcomer category. Todiwala followed up his success by opening a second branch in December 1997 at Battersea in south London with the same vibrant colour schemes and ambience which he hopes will one day put Indian restaurants on the top table of culture, fashion and culinary excellence. In August 2000 he was awarded the MBE for services to the restaurant trade and for education and training, which he takes very seriously. He also has a fast-food restaurant called Parsee in Highgate which serves traditional Parsi cuisine like Mumbai nu Frankie (diced lamb cooked till dry and put in a roti and griddled), and Goan-style sausages Chorise carne de Javali.

In February 1996 came another Indian restaurant with a difference. The *difference* factor was becoming essential now as the market was already very saturated. The new restaurant came complete with a French name, lavish Indian decor and a glamorous launch, bringing yet another new flavour of Indian cuisine to the market. La Porte des Indes (meaning Gateway to India) did not sound at all Indian, and London's Indian restaurant groupies had something else to talk about. But Indian it was. Only La Porte des Indes was serving Indo-French cuisine, and that too in a very British territory – in the heart of Marble Arch – minutes away from the buzzing shopping mecca of Oxford Street. Whatever next, said some critics, until they walked through the door.

Launched by the Blue Elephant Group, which has a chain of highly successful Thai restaurants in Belgium, France, Denmark, Thailand and England, La Porte des Indes brought to London's culinary melting-pot another different ingredient: Indo-French food, or the food found in the French colonies of India. 'When my chairman, Karl Steppe (of the Blue Elephant group), told me in 1993 to go to Pondicherry and do my market research on Indo-French cuisine, I thought it was an absurd idea,' said Sherin Alexander, who with husband Mehernosh Mody, executive chef and co-owner with Sherin of La Porte des Indes, came over from Brussels to take up the challenge.

> I thought I knew India better, but when I reached the homes of Pondicherry I got a pleasant surprise. There really was a cuisine worth exploring. Doing this in Britain, which considers itself the last word on the Indian Empire, was almost outrageous, but we took it on.

The food explored includes the cuisine of the French-Creole communities of Pondicherry, Chandernagore, Yanaon, Mahe and Karikal, where the French settlements were for hundreds of years. Pondicherry, of course, was the major one, and it was here that Sherin was despatched to do some recipe-hunting from some of the *grandes dames* of the region.

The next stage was finding a place. An abandoned ballroom was located, yards from Marble Arch tube station. The property was in a poor condition, having been abandoned for twenty-eight years. It took six months to tear the whole thing apart and give it a total overhaul. Under the capable hands of architect Yves Burton, the place was transformed into a luxurious 320-seater restaurant with a pink sandstone arch flown in from India, a 40-ft cascading waterfall, a white marble staircase linking the upper and lower floors, a shamiana roof on the lower floor, a machan-style jungle bar, and cascades of plants and fresh flowers that all made for a stunning restaurant with a special ambience.

It was the first big-budget Indian restaurant (total expenditure on setting up was £2.5 million) and quite literally made the critics gasp at its unashamed but tasteful opulence. Colourful Indian staff uniforms completed the picture, creating a feel that every night was party night at the La Porte des Indes, according to Sherin Alexander:

The concept was to see India from the eyes of the French, not from the eyes of the British. There was also the idea to get away from the flock wallpaper of Indian restaurants and create a restaurant that was Indian in feel and of a certain high standard.

Backed by the international Blue Elephant chain, the restaurant could afford to splurge on exciting details, paintings and prints, while at the same time being unorthodox and bold. The menus are carefully designed to a high standard with beautiful paintings of the period. There is a special vegetarian menu and even a special tea and coffee menu, each a delight to browse through, says Sherin:

> Our menu shocked our initial customers, who didn't want to struggle through the French names and simply demanded chicken curry and rice. But we explained to them that there was plenty more to try and to experiment. The French in India changed the cuisine to suit them. There was a strong south Indian influence on their food which we have explored in our menu. We are packed every night, so I think there is a taste for it.

La Porte des Indes offered such culinary delights as policha meen from the house of Madame Blanc, the grande dame of Pondicherry, which consists of fresh mullet marinated with green pepper, garlic and shallots, enveloped in banana leaves grilled and served with rougail, a fiery tomato chutney. Also on offer were crevettes assadh, a combination of ocean prawns, mangoes, green chillies, ginger and poppy seeds in a creamy coconut curry. Then again there was Madame Lourde Swamy's ancestral recipe of duck breasts cooked in an exotic blend of indigenous spices (magret de canard pulivaar) and chumude karaikal, sliced beef, stir-fried with onions and whole roasted spices, the method used by the Christian community of Karaikal. Starters like crab Malabar, and calamar à la façon de mahe (stir-fried squid with pepper, garlic and curry leaves) added to the exciting menu, as did the desserts such as yoghurt Chandernagore and Goan bibinca.

La Porte des Indes immediately shot to the top league of Indian restaurants, though Sherin admitted that 60 per cent of her clientele was French, the English still taking their time to settle down to Indo-French cuisine. Hollywood stars like Kim Basinger and Tom Cruise have walked in and been impressed, and the restaurant, because of its sheer size and opulence, is an all-time favourite for weddings and parties. It has already won the Best Indian Restaurant Award from the Curry Club and also Best UK Restaurant and is looking ahead confidently.

A spate of new-look Indian restaurants opened in the years after 1995 – some with European decor, serving a mixture of European and Indian food, with staff drawn from Europe and the subcontinent, while others went in for a minimalist look, whites, pastels and chrome furniture. Most made a point of attracting a smart clientele, not the curry-and-lager crowds, and most were ready to take on trained staff, chefs from India and the modernising of the service. Restaurants like Tamarind, Malabar Junction, Zujuma's, Vama – the Indian Room, the Rupee Room, the Bengal Clipper, to name a few, started to concentrate on attracting an upmarket discerning clientele. At the same time, old and popular restaurants like the Star of India and Khan's of Bayswater, which served traditional Indian food, went in for revamps, smartening up the service and decor to keep up with the new market changes.

Another Mayfair restaurant, Chor Bizarre, a branch of the famous Chor Bazar in Delhi, went in for yet another new look. Started on the site of the old Gaylord restaurant, Chor Bizarre was furnished with artefacts from the flea-markets – chor bazaars of India – and resembled an Aladdin's cave of goodies. Antique furniture, tables, lamps, even a converted four-poster bed, were all arranged to recreate a bazaar ambience. Chor Bizarre's owner, Rohit Khattar, immediately launched himself into the Asian cultural scene and organised book readings and writers' workshops in the restaurant. Chor Bizarre even sponsored theatre festivals bringing the best talent from the Bombay stage to London.

As each restaurant began to assert its individual character, the London culinary map soon began to fill with bold and innovative Indian restaurants. The message from the new Indian restaurant industry clearly was: flock is out, smartness is in – and the Indian restaurant tried to take its place among the smarter restaurants of the capital.

If there was a move to turn minimalist, European and chic, there was also a move to turn trendy and fashionable with an eye on the youth market. And the trendy Indian café was born. One of the pioneers in this field was restaurateur Amin Ali (proprietor of the Red Fort) who started off with a bang, launching an Indian café next door to Sir

Terence Conran's famous Mezzo in Soho. Everyone thought Ali was being suicidal when he told his team: 'I want the crowd that goes to Mezzo to come here.' Mezzo is the place where London's glamorous Soho set hang out. One can chance on a rock star or a film star tucking into coffee and sandwiches at Mezzo. Or one can just see the Soho crowd – artists, directors, technicians, theatre-goers, club musicians and tourists – popping into Mezzo to spend a few hours with friends or in-between work.

It was this crowd that Amin Ali wanted to bring into his café. The project took two years to complete, and designers Fitch were put on the job of creating a trendy Indian café where people could simply relax, eat and enjoy the atmosphere. Soho Spice opened its doors in May 1997, with Apache Indian, the Asian musician who mixes pop, hip-hop, reggae and traditional sounds, doing the honours, and the crowds haven't stopped pouring in.

Decorated in vivid colours – yellow, aquamarine and purple – to bring out the warmth and ambience of the subcontinent, Soho Spice has captured the flavour of India with verve. The colours of Rajasthan are on everything from the menu-card and the table mats to the calling cards and publicity postcards, all in bold spice colours. The waiters and waitresses dressed in brightly coloured khadi kurtas (all bought from Khadi Gram Udyog, Delhi), are a walking advertisement for the khadi cause. And the contemporary Indian art on display (prints selected from the Museum of Modern Art in Delhi) all create an atmosphere that is vibrant, pulsating and uncompromisingly India, at the same time catering to a sophisticated, discerning London crowd.

I knew there was a niche in the Indian restaurant market for a place like this [said Amin Ali]. There are hundreds of Indian restaurants and curry houses. But I wanted to launch a casual dining concept, create an Indian café, as a place where people can come at any time from morning till midnight, a place they can relax with friends and meet people and where they can have a quick bite or a three-course meal, whatever they want.

The location in the heart of Soho couldn't be more ideal. With its melting-pot of theatre, movie houses, sex shops, studios and jazz bars, Soho was the perfect place to create an Indian café with a spicy atmosphere. 'We have become so popular that this café alone is turning over £2 million a year,' said Amin Ali. 'On Fridays and Saturdays we take over a thousand customers.' The place is buzzing every evening and is open late on Fridays and Saturdays till 3 a.m. which brings in the crowds for a bite and drink after a late-night movie or comedy show and after pub closing time. The 200-seater café has a basement bar done in splendid colours – paprika, chilli and saffron – where customers can play the old-time favourite

Indian game, carrom, and snack on bar food like spicy skewers of chicken mirchi and aromatic shami kebabs, samosas and onion bhajis.

The simple but well-chosen menu at Soho Spice offers a range of main courses like tandoori lamb chops, mirch methi murg, and kali mirchi gosht, all reasonably priced under £10. Every month there is also a special cuisine from an Indian state and the year runs through the cuisine from Rajasthan, Bengal, Goa, Hyderabad, the North-West Frontier, Kashmir, Uttar Pradesh, Punjab and Tamil Nadu.

So successful has been the story of Soho Spice that Amin Ali wants to start a chain of Soho Spice cafés with branches in such trendy hot spots as Covent Garden, Islington and Camden. He's even headhunted his chefs from Bangalore and is ready to put Andhra and Kerala cuisine on the café circuit.

But the biggest feather in Amin Ali's cap was the day Fay Maschler of the *Evening Standard* gave a rave review to Soho Spice, on the same day that she gave the thumbs down to Sir Terence Conran's new 240-seater restaurant the Bluebird at King's Road, Chelsea. While Maschler asked 'Have we been Conran-ed?' about the restaurant king who has set the standards for sophisticated Londoners when they dine out, she praised Ali's colourful café venture, set up almost next to Conran's Mezzo. Conran was rated no star (adequate), Ali, one star (good). 'The review made Sir Terence very very angry,' laughs Ali. 'But we're all in the business. He's a good friend, and he knows I'm going to give him competition at Mezzo.' Ali's ambition is clearly to do a Conran, and if the chain of Soho Spice cafés get going, the Bangladeshi from Sylhet can call it a coup.

Apart from Soho Spice, the other cool entry into the new Indian café market was Café Lazeez, started by Zahid Kasim in London's Kensington area in 1992. The restaurant won the prestigious Carlton TV London Restaurant Award for 1998. Again a departure from the curry-house routine, the restaurant was tastefully designed with the downstairs brasserie-style modern and airy with live jazz in the evenings, and the upstairs more formal and subdued. A second branch of Café Lazeez opened in the City in 1998. The Café in Clerkenwell was different in decor, taking on a chrome and glass look that was light, airy and distinctly European.

Catering to the City clientele in the Grade I and II listed building in Clerkenwell, the minimalist design re-established what is already becoming the new trend in Indian restaurants, the all-day dining experience and the smart, professional look. So successful has the chain been that it now has a third branch in Dean Street and a fourth branch in Birmingham at the fashionable and trendy Mail Box.

Café Lazeez has a traditional menu and an evolved menu for those who want to try a bit of fusion. Indo-European fusion foods feature dishes like baked salmon served with chilli and garlic, spicy fish cake, coriander jumbo prawns, and whole red peppers with a filling of fresh garden vegetables and saffron rice, served with roasted tomato cumin sauce. A traditional Indian menu also offers tamarind chilli chicken, avadhi lamb, beetroot lamb and yoghurt tilapia.

The whole concept is to offer healthy Indian food, cooked in an authentic way without too much oil and spices, but retaining its original taste [said Samar Hamid, operations director]. We are on a level with the best French restaurants, and the best cafés. Our food is carefully prepared, freshly prepared and there is nothing like a one-sauce curry.

Hamid, however, regretted that Indian restaurants are still looked down upon as formula curry houses, and never given the status of a French restaurant, though the food, service and ambience could be equally good if not better.

We buy our prime lamb cuts from the same shops, our fish from the best shops, our vegetables from Covent Garden, our wine list is exclusive, and yet when we charge for it in our restaurants, the reaction always is that it's very expensive for an Indian restaurant. It'll take a long time to get rid of the stigma attached to Indian restaurants.

His sentiments were echoed by Namita Panjabi, who has, after her success with Chutney Mary, given a new lease of life to the Veeraswamy by taking it over and modernising it.

Sitting in her elegant and recently refurbished Veeraswamy, which she has transformed into a modern, almost European-style restaurant, Namita regretted the fact that the best of Indian restaurants offering the best dining and culinary experiences still have to underprice their dishes just because the English have a mental block against paying too much in an Indian restaurant.

Every review of my restaurant will always say it is slightly pricey, compared to other Indian restaurants. Why should this be so? After all we are serving gourmet food, we are providing the best ambience and locations. Surely there is a price to pay for it? Top quality Indian restaurants have to work with very low overheads because of this factor.

Namita, always keen to serve the best gourmet food at her restaurants, has on her menu south Indian specialities like Malvani prawn curry with red chilli and coconut cream, Malabar lobster curry, sea bass pollichadu (fillet of sea bass marinated in red Kerala style masala) and north Indian specialities like chicken tikka makhanwala (an Indian version of the CTM) and tandoori salmon.

The food offered is not standard restaurant food, says Namita, but that eaten by gourmet homes in India. With its saffron, purple, gold, green and yellow shades against a glass and chrome background, the new Veeraswamy which opened in 1997 is perhaps representative of the story of the Indian restaurant industry which actually began at the same site seventy-two years earlier. The old Raj furniture, heavy shades and drapery, ornate tables and chairs have gone, to be replaced by elegant contemporary furniture and the vibrant colours of modern India.

In keeping with the bazaar theme, which was becoming very popular, came another spate of restaurants. The former head chef at Soho Spice, Kuldip Singh started his *dhaba* (country-kitchen) style restaurant on Shaftesbury Avenue called Mela. The name itself means 'a fair' and the whole concept of Mela was to do good Indian food at cheap prices. The restaurant has a popular Paratha pavilion and does unbeatable lunchtime deals that keep the customers flowing in, in the heart of theatreland.

Namita Panjabi and sister Camellia Panjabi also launched another restaurant, Masala Zone, offering Indian street food, thalis and other popular dishes at low prices in a trendy setting. With its specially commissioned Warli tribal paintings on the walls, Masala Zone has all the buzz of a contemporary Indian café. Both Mela and Masala Zone have been instant success stories offering quality Indian food at affordable prices in the West End.

But enter the new millennium, and the Indian restaurants had even more to offer. They had grown since their original curry-house days and were clamouring to be included among London's top-class restaurants. The quest had begun for the Michelin star, the ultimate prize for any chef and restaurateur. All eyes were on the Cinnamon Club, the new restaurant to be opened by Iqbal Wahhab. It was Iqbal Wahhab who, as editor of *Tandoori* magazine, had made the famous 'miserable gits' statement about Indian waiters. Now Wahhab wanted to set up his own restaurant, but it was not going to be easy. When Wahhab had been sacked from *Tandoori* magazine, the entire Bangladeshi Restaurateurs Association was up in arms against him and he was isolated.

I was devastated [said Wahhab]. I never thought things would get so out of hand. There was so much bad blood. I was even accused of being in league with the supermarkets to ruin the Bangladeshi-run restaurants. All I had wanted to say was, we've come this far, how do we improve. But they didn't like it. And after all I had done for the industry in all those years at *Tandoori* magazine, I felt really let down.

Iqbal Wahhab found a soulmate in chef Vineet Bhatia (former head-chef of the Star of India). One day, while discussing what a new upmarket Indian restaurant should be like, Vineet said 'no poppadoms' and struck an immediate chord with Iqbal.

Both worked on the menu concept and design. But it wasn't easy working with Iqbal. Finances fell through and a restaurant site in Kensington did not work out. Vineet could not be paid and he had to leave. Eventually Vineet set up Zaika, his fashionable restaurant in Fulham Road with his own style of Indian cuisine served with a European touch. In 2001 he became one of two Indian chefs (the second was Atul Kochhar of Tamarind) to win a coveted Michelin Star. Zaika took up its new residence on Kensington High Street and has become the most fashionable and sought-after Indian restaurant in London today. So famous are Vineet Bhatia's creations that his chocolate samosas are being copied in India and he was asked by British Airways to prepare special cuisine for Concorde's First and Business class passengers which would carry the Vineet Bhatia logo. He was even asked to redesign the crew menu.

And what of Iqbal Wahhab? His story was so interesting that it was even made into a BBC television documentary called *Trouble at the Top*, about ambitious business projects that don't go smoothly. After a few initial let-downs, Wahhab finally managed to acquire a coveted site for his restaurant. It was to be located at the Old Westminster Library, a stone's throw from Parliament and guaranteed to bring in the politicians and media. But there was no easy ride for the former editor of *Tandoori*. Just about everything went wrong. When the builders were in, the money ran out; when the money was raised, the builders found a structural fault, and when that was repaired the money ran out again.

When he advertised for waiters, not one Indian waiter showed up. Wahhab was still facing the wrath of 25,000 Indian waiters upset over the 'miserable gits' statement.

The head chef, Vivek Singh, arrived from India to find he had no kitchen. He went sightseeing instead. Every month of delay led to spiralling debts and finally Wahhab had to re-mortgage his house and hope the restaurant would not leave him bankrupt. Nine eager young chefs arrived from India, to find a restaurant that was still not ready. They, too, went sightseeing. Finally just before D-day, one last let-down: Wahhab was told he could not get a gas connection. The invitations for the opening night had already gone out.

The team of chefs, with typical Indian innovation, said they would cook everything in the tandoor oven (luckily it was only finger foods). Eventually the opening night passed without too many major hiccups and Iqbal Wahhab's poppadom-and-flock-wallpaper-free Cinnamon Club was well on the road by April 2001. The waiters were told that he had a reputation at stake. The industry was watching the man who had made the 'miserable gits' statement. So the waiters would have to smile till their jaws dropped off and treat every guest as if he or she was special.

With head chef Vivek Singh headhunted from India's exclusive Rajvilas Hotel in Jaipur, and menu guidance from two-Michelin-starred chef Eric Chavot of the Capital Hotel whom Wahhab employed as a consultant, the menu was created with a slightly European twist. Wahhab was working full steam towards those elusive Michelin stars.

A few steps from Parliament, the Cinnamon Club had secured an excellent location, that guaranteed a steady supply of parliamentarians ('Tony Blair is the only one who hasn't come,' complains Wahhab) and media. The decor was tasteful with book-lined shelves and smart leather furniture, re-creating both the ambience of the old library and the elegance of a smart restaurant.

When Andrew Lloyd Webber was looking for a place to launch his latest musical *Bombay Dreams*, he chose the Cinnamon Club, and the publicity stood Wahhab well. 'We're breaking even, we're always full and I'm planning to start a branch in New York,' said Iqbal proudly. 'So it was all worth it in the end.' Even Cobra Beer, the sponsors of *Tandoori* magazine, who had fired him after the 'miserable gits' fiasco, had declared a truce and the Cinnamon Club serves Cobra beer in the bar and the restaurant. 'The entente cordiale has been signed,' laughed Iqbal.

But what of the elusive Michelin star? Despite all the hype, Wahhab didn't make it:

I can't say I was not terribly disappointed. Specially in 2003, when we were really hoping we would get it. But things go on. Our restaurant is doing well, and that's the main thing. Good for Vineet Bhatia. He's done very well and I wish him well.

The business of winning and retaining the Michelin star is a tense one. While there were several top-quality Indian restaurants in the mid-nineties, the honour came only in 2001 and went to Vineet Bhatia, chef/owner of Zaika, and Atul Kochhar, head chef of Tamarind.

Vineet Bhatia entered the restaurant scene as late as 1993 when he left Oberoi, Bombay, to join the Star of India as head chef. He remembers how difficult it was for him to adjust to the curry-house menu and routine. 'I didn't even recognise half the things on the menu. Having worked in a five-star hotel in India with a large staff under me, this was a totally different outfit.' Yet Bhatia began improving the menu and changing things at the restaurant – first a 30 per cent change and then nearly the whole menu – earning himself quite a name. After he left the Star of India, he dabbled for a while with the co-ownership of a restaurant in south London. It was called Vineet Bhatia Fine Dining and took off almost immediately. But the restaurant was not professionally run and he left it to join Iqbal Wahhab at the Cinnamon Club. However, that didn't work either as the project was constantly delayed. 'I hadn't been paid, I was living off my credit cards. I had to leave,' said Bhatia. He was able to find financial backers, and Zaika opened in 1999 in Fulham Road, Chelsea. Almost immediately it wowed the critics and in two years won the Michelin star and relocated to Kensington High Street in July 2001. 'I always wanted to do authentic Indian food which was well presented,' said Bhatia. 'The problem with Indian food is we never present it well.' So Bhatia set out to do just that: combine good Indian food with good European-style presentation. And he was off to a winner.

Bhatia also introduced new twists to his menu:

I love colour. I'll do a cream coloured dish and serve it on a beetroot base so the colours stand out – cream and deep red. Or I'll freeze the green chutney and put it on the fish after it has been cooked, and it will simply melt on the hot fish like ice-cream. It's wonderful.

I like to experiment and evolve my cuisine. I don't do fusion – I will never mix sushi and Indian, that is not my style. But I can evolve a chicken tikka, I can evolve a biriani. I do a seafood platter which is actually a seafood khichdi, I call it a risotto. But it is very much an Indian dish with a little innovation.

Bhatia said he was often asked when he started out, whether he wanted to have the best Indian restaurant in London. 'I said no, I wanted to have one of the best restaurants in London, it just happens to be Indian.' A completely hands-on person, 34-year-old Bhatia says he has moved through the system, worked in a curry house and knows what it is like. He still potters in the restaurant kitchen, though being the owner means he cannot be there full-time any more:

I allow my chefs to create as well, and I know that every top chef wants his own restaurant at some time. So I am happy to let them go when they want to. I was a chef once too. It's probably why my staff is very loyal to me and I have never had any problems. In a few years we will be no less than Gordon Ramsay. London can still take in five to eight more Indian restaurants of top quality.

In addition to British Airways, Bhatia is also working as consultant chef to Le Touessrok Hotel in Mauritius where he is creating the menu for an oceanside restaurant called Safran. He is also hoping that Zaika can win a two-star Michelin rating in the near future.

While Bhatia was setting his sights on becoming the next Gordon Ramsay, the tense business of retaining the Michelin star was giving 27-year-old chef Alfred Prasad sleepless nights. Prasad was the sous-chef at the Tamarind restaurant which had won the Michelin star in 2001 with Atul Kochhar as head chef. But Kochhar left in August 2002 to set up his own restaurant and the onus fell on Alfred Prasad to retain the star:

I was really nervous. I changed the menu and had some sleepless nights. But when the announcement came through this year, and we had retained it, it was absolutely brilliant. It's the sort of thing you dream about in India – getting a Michelin star – and it had finally happened.

Prasad had come to London in 1999 from the Maurya Sheraton in Delhi. He had started at Veeraswamy and moved to Tamarind after a few years. Having just six months to retain the Michelin star was a challenge and Prasad put all his skills to the test. 'I enjoy playing around with flavours and creating new dishes,' said Prasad. 'I like to make small innovations like using chives and lemon grass in my traditional prawn dish.' The menu at Tamarind is mainly from north-west India and Prasad, who comes from the south, soon made a few changes. 'I've introduced a seafood moilee which is quite popular and also tried tandoori mushrooms.'

Prasad himself has cooked for a few celebrities. Mel Gibson has enjoyed his lamb chops and Chelsea Clinton loved the hari machli (green fish curry) with coriander and green chilli. He's also cooked for Gordon Ramsay, which the enthusiastic young chef thought was quite an honour.

The Tamarind, under its manager Rajesh Suri, takes the Michelin star very seriously. Suri did not take a day's break when Atul Kochhar left, and he worked non-stop to improve the restaurant and retain the star.

I think we had at least six visits from the Michelin inspectors in the six-month period. They really checked us out. But Alfred has done a superb job in such a short time and it has been very rewarding.

Suri believes firmly that Indian restaurants have been excluded from the Michelin stars because of service and menus:

> It's everything combined. You can have a superb chef producing wonderful things in the kitchen but if it is not served properly, it's wasted. If your waiter does not fill your glass at the right time, know exactly what a regular customer wants and can't explain the menu, then it's useless. We have rigorous training for our staff, we have top professionals choosing our wine list. Everything has to fall in place for the complete dining experience.

Once a month, Rajesh Suri and Alfred Prasad go to a Michelin star restaurant for dinner, just to keep up with the other restaurants. Gordon Ramsay is a regular at Tamarind and always orders the lamb chops. He once invited Suri and Prasad to his restaurant and cooked a six-course meal for them. 'It was absolutely wonderful,' said Prasad. 'The service, the food . . . everything was perfect. . . . You don't become a three-star Michelin Chef for nothing.'

As the race for the Michelin stars goes on, Atul Kochhar, former head chef of Tamarind, will also be trying to retain his star in his own restaurant, Benares, which opened in April 2003.

Kochhar, born and brought up in Jamshedpur in eastern India (where his father had a catering business), joined the Oberoi Hotel in Delhi and was headhunted from there as head chef for Tamarind in 1994:

> I started with just one chef and went on to win the Michelin star. I was delighted when I got the star, but I had never been obsessed with getting it. My job was to bring the true flavour of Indian food to my restaurant and I think I did that.
>
> It was a long journey to get here. It was a process of learning on my part. The market has changed a lot over the years, people are understanding the spices. They are understanding the different flavours of Indian cuisine. I came here for three years and never went back. It's been very fascinating.

At Tamarind, Kochhar prepared mainly north Indian food, but at his own restaurant he wants to have a selection of regional Indian cuisine. Particularly fascinating for him is the cuisine of east India, particularly Bengal and Orissa.

> I want to present a melange of Indian food, I want to change the menus often and I want to be regional and seasonal. When I'm cooking Kerala food, I want to get into the heart of a Keralite, when I'm cooking Bengali food I want to get into the Bengali kitchen. The best Bengali food is what is served in the houses in Bengal cooked by the *boudi* (sister-in-law/lady of the house). I was so surprised when I came here and found that though the restaurants were owned by

Bangladeshis, none of them actually served Bengali food.

Kochhar has been travelling extensively in India researching his book, which is due soon, and hunting for new recipes which he will be trying at Benares. The decor of Benares is minimalist with the feel of the inner courtyard of a haveli in Benares. Designers Ou Baholyalhin, who have designed Thai restaurants before, have worked with Kochhar's ideas of a water feature, the colour saffron and a courtyard theme. 'I want people to feel they are dining in a contemporary modern Indian restaurant, but at the same time eating traditional Indian food.'

Kochhar himself is in the kitchen – 'there's no other place I can be' – designing, creating and closely supervising the menu. He has hired a team of five chefs including the sous chef from the Oberoi Uday Vilas Palace. 'I believe in letting a chef create his dishes, so I will give them the freedom to do so. I don't believe in stepping on anyone's toes.'

There's no hint of fusion in Kochhar's kitchen. 'I don't do fusion,' he says vehemently:

The most I may ever do is try to blend Indian food from the east and the west – maybe do an eastern fish curry with south Indian spices, but that too very very rarely. Indian food has such a variety, and these are the flavours I want to bring out.

Kochhar says he once ate a thali in Jaipur which had about five different vegetarian dishes. They were all made from chick-pea flour, but they all had their individual flavour. That was the sort of variety he wanted to present:

I think the Michelin inspectors have begun to understand Indian food now. They understand the concept of Indian food, and that it has to be shared. One person cannot order a rogan josh and eat just that. That is not the way Indian food is eaten. I think they have now become familiar with the taste and presentation. And I think many more Indian restaurants will get Michelin stars in future. They are looking for enthusiasm, dedication and consistency. When I got the Michelin star I was congratulated by other fellow chefs like Udit Sarkhel [formerly of Bombay Brasserie and now successfully running his own restaurant Sarkhel's in South London] and they said it was a great step forward for Indian food.

He is, of course, hoping to win a Michelin star in his new restaurant. Benares will be located in Berkeley Square, a short distance from his old restaurant Tamarind. Kochhar knew his restaurant had to be in Mayfair, because he was familiar with the area and because the regular diners in the area knew him. 'Competition is always fierce,' he laughs. 'But I think there's room for all of us.'

The heat in these kitchens is definitely on the rise. As top chefs from India hone their culinary skills, the pots and pans are sizzling as Indian restaurants vie for the Number One slot. From curry houses to Michelin star restaurants, the rogan josh and chicken tikka have travelled a long way. For lovers of spice it can only be good news.

8

Invading the Pubs

Deep in the Hertfordshire countryside, the residents of Bulbourne and Tring have something special to look forward to every week: a curry in their local pub. For even here deep in the country, the taste for curry runs strong. The Grand Junction Arms, the local pub at Bulbourne, is known to residents as the 'Curry Pub'. Here pub landlord Simon Sturl serves up the curries regularly and has the locals trooping in for more as curries take over the last British bastion: the pub.

Every day is curry day at the Grand Junction Arms, with Sturl laying on a choice of several curries which he cooks himself. A self-taught cook, Sturl says he started with one curry a night, and has now mastered recipes as varied as pork sorpotel from Goa, beef malai tikka (beef cooked in cream), chicken cooked with cream and coconut and fish dishes like machchi methi. He even stirs up regular dishes like a lamb do-piaza, but tries to keep away from the formula curries, and standard chicken tikka masala. 'I avoid the curry house range,' said Sturl, 'and try to make my menu varied, and more regional.'

Sturl serves up a regular lunchtime buffet which has curry on the menu and for the evenings does some special dishes from his regional range which are slightly more expensive. Like all pubs, Sturl operates a blackboard system, and lists the special dishes of the day.

Thursdays are themed curry nights and on these days he tries to do something special as well. Often he explores regional south Asian and south-east Asian cooking on these nights, trying out Indonesian and other cuisine which is similar to Indian food. He has found these to be immensely popular.

Sturl has been serving curries in his pubs for the past twelve years, and is himself a keen fan. He has been running the Grand Junction for the past five years, but previously owned the Queen's Head pub at Long Marston, which he had made famous for its curries. 'I started with one curry on Thursday nights, but they grew so popular that I threw out the steak and chips in favour of Indian dishes.' Some of the customers from Long Marston still drive down a few miles to Bulbourne for his curries. The Grand Junction Arms was one of the finalists for the Ethnic Food Publican Awards in 2002.

The pub itself is bigger than the Queen's Head and Sturl has found it challenging to keep up with the demand. 'Because we have a large garden, we are specially popular in the summers and we serve nearly 500 covers a week. At least 400 of these covers are for curries, the rest for regular pub grub.'

In summer Sturl likes to do barbecues in the evening. He usually does a tandoori chicken, marinated in spices and cooked over charcoal, and served up with a salad. The most popular are simple salads with tomato, chilli and coriander leaf or rice-based salads. Poppadoms, naan bread, bhajis and samosas, with a selection of dips and chutneys, are also on offer. A keen cook, and one who likes experimenting, Sturl has created new accompaniments such as pickled fish, spicy mackerel or trout. 'I'll have them all converted at the Grand Junction soon,' he says with easy confidence.

And if the British are looking for curries even in country pubs, can the regular pubs in big cities avoid the curry craze? Not exactly. Check out the Punch and Judy, the popular and buzzing pub in the heart of Covent Garden and there on the blackboard along with other dishes of the day will be the inevitable chicken tikka masala, or chicken korma. The same is true in most pubs. Along with the roast chicken and chips, or the cod and chips will be lamb rogan josh or simply chicken curry and rice. Six times out of ten these will have been cooked using ready-made sauces, as only a few dedicated pubs make the effort to cook it authentically. But the demand is always there, whether it's out of a jar or cooked from scratch.

It is estimated that around 6,500 pubs all over the country serve Indian food, which goes to show that pub landlords see the potential in offering a chicken tikka with a pint to the locals.

In the heart of Coventry, just over a hundred miles from London, people queue up for curry at another unusual place – a balti pub. For Pele's Balti Pub owned by Perminder Bains, or Pele to his friends, is the first full Indian pub serving Indian food, owned by Indians and having an Indian theme and decor. He hopes it will be the first of many similar pubs soon to be launched in Britain. In a tie-up with Roger Myers, who started the Café Rouge chain, Pele wants to bring the first Indian pub chain to the country, taking over the all-English pub, lock, stock and balti.

Born in Kenya, Pele returned to Hoshiarpur with his parents in 1965 at the age of eight. His father, a building contractor, remained in India for four or five years and Pele was thirteen when the family moved to Coventry. After school in Coventry, Pele went on to study electrical engineering.

In 1973 he got a job as an electrical engineer in Jaguar cars and also started working part-time in the evenings at an Irish pub. He became friendly with the owner, Jimmy O'Keefe and found that he enjoyed the job tremendously. Jimmy O'Keefe kept telling Pele that he should become a full-time pub landlord. But in those days the law required that pub landlords had to be married. Pele had not yet found a partner. On a trip to India in 1974, Pele met Jatinder, who also came from Hoshiarpur. They had an arranged marriage and returned to Coventry in 1974. He now fulfilled the legal requirement to own a pub. Again at O'Keefe's insistence, Pele took over his first pub in 1975, becoming the first Indian to own one.

He tried his hand at two or three pubs until 1981, when he heard that the William IV in Coventry was looking for a new owner. It was in 1985 that Perminder Bains and his wife Jatinder took over the William IV pub on Foleshill Road. The pub was a fairly run-down one, not too far from the local Asian shopping area. Brewers Mitchells and Butlers thought it would be a good idea to have an Indian landlord in a largely Indian area.

But Pele was not content with serving pies and scampi and chips. With a cash injection from the brewers he thoroughly refurbished and extended the pub. Next it was time to bring in the korma. 'Why don't we put chicken curry on the menu?' he asked wife Jatinder one day. 'Don't be silly,' was her response. 'It'll never sell.' The Bainses had been used to English neighbours who closed the window whenever they cooked. But Pele was undeterred. He put up a sign on the blackboard saying 'Chicken curry and rice'. Jatinder did the rest, and it was a hit. That day no one ordered scampi and chips. Pele knew it was the way to go. Soon he brought in lamb curry, then chicken tikka and found his menu was gradually changing.

Slowly the range had to be increased as Pele and Jatinder found that the demand was continuously growing. One night Pele told Jatinder that there was a real market for curries out there and they could win it if they worked hard. The couple took a trip to India, staying with a friend who was in the army. The friend arranged cooking lessons for Pele. Now he was really in the field. Pele still goes to India three or four times a year, continuously looking for fresh ideas and recipes. Every holiday is a working holiday, as he inevitably gets into the kitchens and persuades the chefs to part with their recipes. Back in Coventry, Pele and Jatinder taught their staff what they had learnt in India, and the pub could now offer even more variety.

Throwing out the traditional cod and chips from his menu was something Pele did with ease, earning himself several awards and recognition on television and in the print media. The awards flowed in: the Best Pub Food Award, both nationally and in the Midlands, the Nestlé Food Award, Pure Genius Award, Patak's Restaurant of the Year Award, and Uncle Ben's Curry Pub of the Year Award. Pele's pub was listed by the Curry Club and the *Egon Ronay Guide*, and won the Taj Curry Pub of the Year. So popular was Pele's food that brewers Bass started taking notice, and thought they could use his food to attract people to other pubs with a declining clientele. Another pub, the Burnt Post, in a well-heeled area of Coventry, ordered Indian food from Pele's kitchen and advertised their own Indian night.

One evening in 1993, when Britain was still in recession, and attendance at restaurants and pubs was low, pots of chicken tikka masala, chicken badshai, zafrani, basmati rice and other delectables were cooked in Pele's kitchen, loaded on to vans and driven to the Burnt Post, where nearly 250 seats were sold for the special night. An Irish band played live while customers tucked into their curries and Bass brewery executives smiled in satisfaction as they saw the booming business. Pele had scored an Indian coup in the heart of a recession.

As pubs up and down the country tried to copy him, Pele decided to go a step further and do things on his own. He now wanted a chain of pubs bearing his name and catering his menu. It was time to translate the achievement in Coventry up and down the country from the south-east to Scotland. Negotiations with Roger Myers proved successful and at the end of July 1998, Pele and Myers launched the balti pub chain. Pub operator Punch Taverns offered Pele £80,000 to head a nationwide franchise scheme, and the company planned a further £40 million investment in pub properties to set up the balti chain.

First to be revamped and refurbished was Pele's starting ground, the William IV at Coventry. The pub was renamed Pele's Balti Pub and the designers spent weeks in India absorbing the colours of the subcontinent to give it a total revamp. 'I wanted to recreate the village atmosphere of Punjab, where I come from,' said Pele. The walls are painted in vivid blues, pinks and yellows and each wall is named after a particular spice and carries the history of the spice. The walls are a veritable tourist's guide to India. A medley of objects are framed – from photographs of the Kumbh Mela, to portraits of villagers, miniature paintings, contemporary Indian art, even a collection of *rakhis* – all bringing out the buzz of life in India. Even the music playing in the pub is a collection of Indian film songs, Indian folk songs, and Indian fusion. Colonial Cousin meets Apache Indian meets Zakir Hussain.

The colourful menu card is a pub diner's dream. A variety of Indian food is on offer from balti chicken zaffrani to chana punjabi and paneer makhanwala. There are exotic birianis, exciting thalis, and to round off there are matka kulfis. The food is good Punjabi food – the region from where Pele comes and the cuisine he knows – and every effort is made to serve it as authentically as you would get in Hoshiarpur.

For the unadventurous, Pele also offers a selection of plaice and chips, scampi and chips and chicken and chips. But it is usually Pele's balti dishes – all served up in little karahis and with naan and salad – that the mixture of English and Asian clients (many of them turbanned Sikhs) can be seen tucking in to.

Midlands is the heart of balti cuisine [said Pele], so I simply had to serve balti. The food is broadly the cuisine of the Himalayan regions of Pakistani Kashmir and Punjab. I plan to go a step further and serve from little copper *baltis* as well, which is probably how the word balti came into being.

Pele also plans thali evenings, and live music nights. He has already contacted a supplier in Delhi to send him around 400 karahis and small copper baltis. For Pele the presentation is as important as the food:

> I think there's a lot we can do. But the best thing is that we are still a pub and not a restaurant. People can sit here for as long as they like with a drink and nobody will rush them. They have to order their food at the bar like all pubs and need not eat if they don't want to. We are not rigid like a restaurant, we are essentially a pub. And our prices are also pub prices.

All priced at less than a fiver, Pele's reasonable prices make the place even more attractive. He even does a special deal: a pint and a balti meal for just £5.50 – an offer that most pub-goers don't miss out on. He also does some exotic Oriental drinks such as cherbert tokhum – a sweet basil-flavoured, aphrodisiacal concoction, and cherbert pani, a sparkling infusion of coriander and peppermint.

Co-owner and financier Roger Myers, who created the successful Café Rouge chain, is confident that the Balti pub chain will take off in a big way, repeating its Coventry success:

> I do not see why the balti pub should not become as big as Café Rouge. The idea is that we will help the tenants who are already there to set up their own outlets. It is different to a traditional managed restaurant chain.

Pele himself would like to take the logo nationally and to Europe as well. He is looking at venues in Scotland, Brighton, and even in London. All the pubs will have the same menu, the same decor and the same ambience. Pele says he would like to create an Indian pub chain that would put Indian food in a different category altogether by promoting it through a pub chain. In India he has been awarded the Hind Rattan Award, an award for enterprising and successful expatriate Indians.

'I've been collecting recipes since 1981,' says Pele. 'I still have many in stock. Jatinder and me are planning to bring out a cook book soon.' As for new recipes, he says he always manages to get a few every time he visits India, even if he has to bribe, talk or charm his way into getting them. He would love to open a similar chain in India and provide good quality authentic food in a pub atmosphere. But that's the long-term future. For the moment he's going in search of a giant copper balti which he would like to hang outside his pub, as a symbol of Midlands balti cuisine.

Pele isn't the only one who runs an Indian pub. Down in Southall in west London, a place known as mini-India for a long time, visitors from India could until recently pay in rupees for a drink at the Glassy Junction. Now with the fluctuating exchange rate, this is no longer possible. But the Glassy Junction is very different from Pele's Balti Pub because, unlike Pele's, which is pretty much a mainstream pub with a large white clientele, you wouldn't see a white face at the Glassy Junction. You wouldn't even see

too many women or families, for that matter, for the
Glassy Junction is almost exclusively a male Sikh
pub for the local Sikh population of Southall. The
food served is Indian, the beer is Indian and the
music is Indian – bhangra to be precise.

But the Glassy has no wish to change its image,
and wants to remain a pukka Sikh pub, for the
locals and by the locals. The pub is decorated on
the outside with giant murals of Sikh bhangra
dancers. This is the watering hole of the
community that has made this suburb of London
near Heathrow airport their home for nearly the
past forty years. Opposite the pub is the office of
the Punjabi newspaper, *Des Pardes*, and many an
evening is spent in the pub by local Punjabis
discussing Indian politics, dreaming of the *pind*
(village), and tanking up with beer, chicken
tandoori and bhangra music.

Even Wembley has an Indian pub, which has
been drawing in crowds since it opened in 1997.
The Club 182 on Preston Road is tastefully
decorated with a typical clubhouse atmosphere.
The walls are covered with black and white
photographs of old cricketing heroes, maharajas
and their entourage, Indian leaders from the
freedom struggle and other Raj memorabilia. A
giant screen plays Bollywood film songs and the
pub is full to capacity every evening with a mixed
white and ethnic clientele. Inevitably, the cricket
season means the pub gets packed with India
supporters and the mood is euphoric when Sachin
Tendulkar and Rahul Dravid get going with the bat.

Miles from the ethnic ambience of Wembley and Southall, Joanna Rainbird finds there's no getting away from chicken tikka masala even in Kent, in England's garden county. Joanna and her husband, Michael, who run the Rose and Crown pub, find that chicken is also an ideal meat to marinate for those long summer evening barbecues. Joanna serves her customers barbecued chicken (which she marinates in yoghurt, cumin seed, coriander leaf and lemon juice), accompanied with cucumber and mint raita and a vegetable or salad. It is always a hit.

Apart from summers, the Rainbirds do curries at least once a month. They always have a good response, she says. 'People like the spicy food, currys are always popular.' Joanna, who has picked up her Indian cooking from reading magazines and books and watching television, says she usually serves chicken curry, lamb curry and prawn curry.

What started with serving the occasional samosa and onion bhajis at pubs has grown into a full-fledged curry industry as pub-owners realise there is business in curries. In Scotland, at Murphy's Pakora Bar – a jazzy bar with lots of brass, mirrors and glass in the heart of Glasgow's West End – they serve haggis pakoras, black pudding pakoras and spam fritter pakoras, catering for the twenty-something crowd that come in for a drink and a snack. The bar does fifty types of pakoras and is an institution in itself. With thirty beers on draught, the bar with forty seats upstairs and forty downstairs does a roaring business in beer and pakoras as Scottish youngsters enjoy the blending of traditional Scottish and Indian dishes.

Meanwhile, in a village in the heart of Somerset, a quintessentially English country pub, the Halfway House, has on its menu rogan josh and chicken masala, for a special occasion and the inevitable curry night.

They are even serving curries in a pub on a remote windswept island off the coast of Scotland, in Port Askaig, in the Inner Hebrides, which is only accessible by a long ferry-ride from the mainland. David and Ruby Graham, who run the Ballygrant Inn in Port Askaig, found that Scottish islanders like to go out for curries when they visit the mainland. So they thought they would start serving it to them locally. 'The islanders love their curry. And now they don't have to go out to get it any more,' said Ruby Graham.

The Grahams had developed a taste for curries when they lived in Glasgow, and were keen to start cooking it. When they took over the Ballygrant Inn in 1990, they took the plunge. Armed with *The Encyclopaedia of Indian Cooking*, some of Madhur Jaffrey's cook books and a collection of other restaurant recipe books, the couple went to work in their kitchen.

Spices and ingredients were easily picked up from Glasgow and a local Asian wholesaler, and the couple began experimenting with the new dishes. A range of curries appeared on the menu – lamb, chicken, vegetable, pork – and before long business was thriving. The pub even went on to win the Uncle Ben's Curry Pub of the Year in 1994, and still serves curry regularly on its menu. 'We are sure that our curries, with that genuine taste of the East, have helped us win recognition of our menus,' said the proud Scottish couple, who have been married for twenty years and eaten curry for as many.

From country pubs in windswept Scotland, to those in the heart of London's West End, curry is definitely on the menu. As curries put the buzz into many pubs, brewers have begun to realise that there is money in curry. And as long as the tills are ringing, it won't be last orders for curries for a while.

9

Balti and Beyond

In India *balti* means a bucket. In Britain it means a range of Indian food. I felt I could not do justice to this book if I did not check out the famous balti. So, with my seven-year-old daughter moaning in the back seat: 'Mama says I have to eat baltis. Why do I have to eat baltis?' (her knowledge of baltis being confined to buckets) and other such prattle, we headed up the M1 from London for that famous balti destination – Birmingham.

For it was here in Birmingham that 'balti' was born, a dish that soon achieved cult status, especially in the eighties, leading to a spate of balti restaurants all over the country. Today Birmingham is as famous for its baltis as its Repertory Theatre, and the city website has detailed references to the numerous balti restaurants that dot the area.

Our destination was a particular area in south Birmingham which is referred to as 'the balti triangle'. It is the area comprising Sparkhill, Sparkbrook, Ladypool and Moseley, an area with a large population of Pakistanis and Mirpuri Kashmiris and the home of balti. In the tiny lanes and shabby streets dotted with ethnic shops selling bright sequined salwar kameezes and saris, bangles, shoes, south Asian vegetables, fish and halal meat, are the balti restaurants. There are apparently more than fifty restaurants in this two-mile zone alone, most open until late at night and always buzzing.

I dropped into Adil's, one of the oldest balti restaurants in the area and winner of several awards including the Curry Club Best Balti Restaurant Award in 1999. With simple pine-stripped walls and glass-top tables with the menus displayed underneath, it looked like it had been stuck in a time-frame from the seventies.

Adil himself is a 21-year-old who helps his brother Rashid run the restaurant that was started by their father, Mohammed Arif. 'I was actually named after the restaurant,' laughs Adil. 'When my dad bought this restaurant, it was already called Adil. I was born after he set it up, so I was called Adil after the restaurant.'

Mohammed Arif has retired from full-time management of the restaurant. He came down from the local mosque to talk about how balti came to Birmingham. An impressive man with a white beard and traditional Pakistani clothes, Mohammed Arif claims to be the person who invented balti and regrets not having registered it as a cuisine. The family came to Britain from the Pakistan-side of Kashmir in 1968. They first went to Bradford where they worked in the textile mills. In 1972, they moved to Birmingham where an uncle was running a restaurant. Working in his uncle's restaurant, Mohammed Arif learnt the ropes of the restaurant business. In 1977, he bought Adil's and started his own restaurant.

> Those days there were hardly any restaurants in the area – just two or three [said Arif]. Even there, they would pre-cook the meal and simply warm it up and serve it to the customer. I had seen restaurants in Peshawar in Pakistan where they cooked in a karahi and served the food hot in the karahi itself. That is what I wanted to do. I wanted to serve fresh cooked food in the karahi and start something new. So I started serving karahi gosht.

Arif got karahis from Pakistan and started the new menu in his restaurant. Soon he was able to get the karahis manufactured locally and this was the start of the curry-house fare in Birmingham. 'We used to serve it with freshly made naan bread and it was an immediate hit. We had seven to eight big tables and people sat at the tables and ate the hot food.'

Arif has his own theory about how the karahi dish got the name balti. (Over the next few days I was to hear several theories about the same question.) According to Arif, the English could not pronounce 'karahi' so it was causing a problem. An English friend of his suggested he give it some other name which was easy to pronounce. 'I just said "balti" and he repeated "balti" after me easily and that's how it came to be.'

Now [he says], balti has been taken to ridiculous lengths. Everything is balti, you have balti this and balti that and even balti kulfi ('Why, even my restaurant serves it'). Every restaurant is balti, kebabs are balti, tandoori is balti. Nothing has been spared. They have flogged the balti horse till there's nothing left any more.

Arif says the competition is stiff with over 200 restaurants in Birmingham alone. Most, he claims, are not authentic. 'Balti is karahi, nothing more. It is a dish cooked in Kashmir and in Pakistan, and served with naan.'

Arif remembers the queues that used to form outside his restaurant in the eighties:

People were prepared to wait outside in the cold till they got a table. I had a lady from Pakistan who helped me in the kitchen and she used to make the most delicious naans and karahi gosht. She taught me a lot and our staff even now are trained on exactly the same recipes and style of cooking. All my old customers return to my restaurant. I have served some of them when they came with their parents and now they are coming with their children.

Sitting at his tables were three English families, all in their sixties with grandchildren in tow. 'They are all my old customers,' said Arif.

Adil serves a variety of baltis ranging from chicken spinach and chicken mushroom balti to balti meat chana, balti meat spinach mushroom, and even a balti meat egg. There are rogan josh baltis, kurma baltis, dhansak baltis and masala baltis. Basically, any combination you like can be cooked as a balti dish and served with a variety of naans in all flavours and many sizes.

The specialities of the balti restaurants in Birmingham – which set them apart from the curry houses in London and the rest of Britain – were two things: the food would be served in a big karahi and the naans were made a size that don't exist anywhere else. Most Birmingham balti restaurants serve a medium naan (that's the size of two normal naans), a family naan (the size of three normal naans) and a table naan (a naan that literally fills the table) and this is shared by everybody. Its roots are probably tribal. In the north-west frontier provinces of Pakistan and Afghanistan, they do make a giant-size naan or bread which is called khubz. The family naans of Birmingham are probably derived from the same roots.

At the Imran restaurant on Ladypool Road, a buzzing slightly upmarket place with a more contemporary decor, I asked to see how the naans were made. The owner, Afzal Butt, was more than happy to show me around the kitchen. The giant naans were rolled out on the table top and then lifted deftly on to a full-size pillow. It was on the pillow that it was taken into the tandoor and stuck on the sides of the oven. Normal naans and tandoori rotis are put on a small rolled cloth with which they are taken to the tandoori oven. Here, in

Birmingham, it was travelling on a pillow. The 'pillow naans' were then doused with a touch of ghee and served hot. The sight of the giant naans being carried across the restaurant with a flourish accompanied by the sizzling dishes in their karahis all made for a pretty colourful presentation. It was easy to see why this dish had become so popular and become such a Brummie trademark.

Afzal Butt of Imran's is a genial man who is proud of his newly refurbished restaurant. His is one of the oldest establishments in Birmingham and I was soon to hear Butt's own theory about how the balti got its name:

My first restaurant in this area was called Gazala which I started in 1970. We served traditional Pakistani food from Lahore and it was very popular. Our naans and kebabs were famous. There was so much pressure on the restaurant that we opened another restaurant in 1977. This was Imran's, which I called after my eldest son. We served karahi gosht and karahi chicken, which are typical dishes from Lahore. But people couldn't pronounce it. I had a friend called Harry Smith and he said, 'What is this karahi, I can't pronounce it.' He started playing around with my name saying, 'You are Butt, this is Butt's curry, Brummie curry,' and then he just said 'balti'. And he could pronounce it fine. Well that's how balti came to stay and the name was born. In a way I gave my name to the dish.

Not everyone may agree with Butt's version, but at least both Arif and he agreed on one thing: the balti was no different from the karahi.

Situated in the busy and buzzing Ladypool Road, with kebab shops and balti restaurants almost back-to-back, Imran's has had a successful run. It has managed to pull in a celebrity clientele and has major expansion plans. Television presenter Rolf Harris, violinist Vanessa Mae, actor Art Malik, comedian Frank Skinner, the entire Pakistan cricket team and even the famous *qawwali* singer, the late Nusrat Fateh Ali Khan, have eaten at Imran's. Cabinet minister Clare Short has a special table where she usually sits at Imran's and even the former Pakistan Prime Minister, Nawaz Sharif, has tried the peshawari naans, kebabs and balti gosht available at Imran's.

Butt is proud that his two sons, Imran and Usman, are taking the restaurant business forward and have new ideas. Usman has an MSc in catering from Sheffield and is keen to take the restaurant upmarket and out of the curry-house bracket. 'I am inspired by the way Indian restaurants have come up in London and I do see the need to modernise,' said Usman. 'We've come this far and are doing very well but we have to go further.' 'When we started in 1970, it was out of necessity,' said Mohammed Afzal Butt. 'We were doing a good job, but we were not professionally trained. The second generation is going to do that for us,' he added.

A gleaming sweet shop filled with freshly prepared Indian sweets is attached to the restaurant, which also has an open kitchen where the kebabs are being made. 'We are almost packed to capacity over the weekends and things have been going well,' said Butt. 'Hopefully it will continue like this.'

Less than a quarter of a mile away from Imran's is another famous Birmingham balti restaurant, the Royal Naim, situated on Stratford Road. Owner Mohammed Nazir came from Pakistani Kashmir in 1984 and set up the restaurant in 1989. He naturally had a third theory about baltis. Everyone inevitably did. In fact there were so many theories that Kipling himself would be challenged to name a winner and include it in his *Just So Stories* as 'How the Balti Got its Name'.

Nazir himself had a completely no-nonsense approach to the topic. He simply stated that in the part of Kashmir that he came from – known variously as Azad Kashmir (Free Kashmir) by the Pakistani government, or Pakistan-occupied Kashmir by the Indian government – a karahi was also known as a balti. 'The balti is the dish it is served in,' said Nazir. 'In Kashmir we call it balti.' 'But what do you call a bucket?' I asked him. 'Balti,' he said. And that was that.

Nazir's restaurant was obviously very popular. A huge group of twenty beefy-looking, heavily tattooed men were tucking into the family naans and steaming hot karahis. A steady stream of people entered – English grandparents with children in tow, an Asian couple with a young boy and some youngsters enjoying a weekend lunch out. The wall of the restaurant was decorated with murals of the Dal Lake in Srinagar in Kashmir.

Ironically, the diet of Indian Kashmiris from Srinagar and the Valley is very different from the balti cuisine of the north-west frontier. The Kashmiris from the Valley eat delicacies like gushtaba (a sort of meatball curry) and haaq (spinach cooked with delicate spices) and drink a flavoured tea called kahwa which is a must in all Kashmiri restaurants in India. Their dishes are cooked with almonds and raisins and are fairly mild. Here in Birmingham, the cuisine of the north-west frontier and Mirpur had evolved into its own version of Kashmiri food and eventually into what is now known as balti cuisine.

Royal Naim, like most other balti restaurants, had a glass-top table with a menu displayed under it, and served a variety of baltis – from jalfrezies and kormas to do-piaza, tikka masala, *pathia* (a dish cooked with sweet and sour sauce), and garlic chilli baltis. Lamb, chicken, vegetables or prawns could be cooked in any of these styles and served in a karahi. There was even a tropical balti which included lamb, chicken, prawns and vegetables all thrown together into a karahi and served.

My collection of balti theories was not yet over. There was another floating theory whose source could not be traced. I had heard it mentioned off and on in connection with balti. This one was bordering on the political. This was the claim that balti was the cuisine of Baltistan, an area of Pakistan which is currently fighting for independence and statehood. This was probably the mother of all balti theories.

The troubled political history of this area made the theory even more remarkable. Gilgit and Baltistan are two areas in northern Pakistan close to the Karakoram ranges and the best place for treks to Mount K2. The area is often known as Little Tibet because of its close cultural affinity to Ladakh. The religion here was once Buddhism and is now predominantly Islam. And here lies the irony: there is no evidence that the area of Baltistan with its de facto capital in remote Skardu in north Pakistan ever had anything like the cuisine we can see today in Ladypool Road and Sparkbrook.

The area of Gilgit and Baltistan went to Pakistan after partition and is now in a region described as the Northern Area. The region feels unjustly treated and there is a small movement for independence from Pakistan. The area is probably closer in affinity and cuisine to Tibet than Kashmir. So the theory that balti comes from Baltistan was rubbished by those restaurateurs who come from Lahore like Butt, and those who come from Mirpur, like Arif. 'There's no such thing as the cuisine of Baltistan,' roared Arif when I put this theory to him. 'Where is Baltistan anyway? Everybody is saying their own thing. I can tell you that it is simply the food from Pakistan, from Peshawar and the North West.'

I was referred to a restaurant called K2 in Moseley which had a map of Baltistan on its walls and served Kashmiri baltis. But here, too, there were no takers for the theory. Even the map of Baltistan had been removed in the restaurant's refurbishment.

The manager, Mr Niam, wasn't himself sure about the origin of the word 'balti' but he put me on to Navid Haq, an old-timer in the restaurant who completely dismissed the theory:

It is a north Indian dish, from Punjab. There is no connection between the area of Baltistan and the cuisine. Basically the meat is cooked in dhabas (roadside stalls) in Punjab and (Mirpuri) Kashmir in a karahi and is served straight. It is just the name for the metal wok. I have no idea how the karahi came to be known as balti, but in this country so many things evolved over the years to cater to the English taste and pronunciation.

The Bangladeshis cooked dishes called chicken masala, which don't exist in India. The Anglo-Indian influence led to some new dishes. Somewhere along the way the karahi became the balti.

Haq, a Mirpuri Kashmiri himself, said the food of the region was closer to Pakistani Punjab and that is what was served in Birmingham.

With no solution to my question, and things beginning to get heated between the Mirpuri

Kashmiris and the Pakistanis all staking their claim to inventing balti, it was best to drop the matter. After all, wherever it came from and whoever created it, the bottom line was that it had worked.

Balti has spread from Birmingham to the rest of Britain. It has been copied by supermarkets who made the curries and food manufacturers who had turned out balti pastes. I have even seen balti in a fashionable upmarket restaurant in Bangalore in India, and I've been told Delhi has a few as well. Balti cookbooks have sold thousands of copies and the cuisine is part of the Birmingham map.

Which is not to say that Birmingham means only balti. The Mailbox, Birmingham's stunning lifestyle development, with its fashionable restaurants on the top floor, also has a Café Lazeez, a branch of the restaurant in London. The smart upmarket restaurant with its fusion cuisine offers the other side of the Indian dining experience in the Midlands.

As one goes further north from Birmingham, the balti houses soon turn back into curry houses. In Bradford, in the heart of Yorkshire, though the population is nearly the same ethnic mix as Birmingham – Mirpuri Kashmiri and Pakistani – the balti is not so visible. It appears in menus, in between the karahi dishes, but Bradford stakes its reputation purely on its kebab and karahi cuisine.

No surprises then, that one of the most popular curry houses in Bradford, the Karachi, has just celebrated its fortieth birthday. The complete no-frills, no-fuss curry house has continued in the same tradition as when it started and has no plans to change. Its range of karahi lamb, karahi chicken, tarka daal, kebabs and biriani are famous in Bradford and beyond. The Karachi has formica tables, no tablecloths and cutlery only if you ask for it. Most people simply tear their chapattis which are supplied in a steady stream to the tables and dip into their curries with it. Dishes still cost under a fiver each and the Karachi has a continuous supply of visitors, from students and young men looking for a Friday night curry, to families and couples.

Once the photographer, David Bailey, came to the Karachi and took photographs of the restaurant. He wanted to take a photograph of chef proprietor Mumrez Khan. But Khan, who was busy cooking for his lunchtime customers, refused to be photographed. It was only later that he was told that the photographer was David Bailey and that people paid a fortune to be photographed by him. But Mumrez said it didn't matter. David Bailey sent Mumrez Khan the photographs of the restaurant he had taken anyway, and he has filed them away. It is the typical attitude of the curry house: everyone is treated the same and the food is what matters.

Bradford's other famous curry houses include the Nawab (former cricket captain Imran Khan's favourite), the Bengal Brasserie (this one is Bangladeshi-run) and the Mumtaz. Standard curry-house fare here is usually kebabs, karahi chicken, shahi paneer and tarka daal. Occasionally there is tandoori fish as well. Bradford's curry houses have never felt the need to change.

Imran Khan still claims that the best kebabs come from Bradford. Both the Indian and Pakistani cricket teams regularly travel up to Bradford if they are playing in Leeds. And India's master batsman, Sachin Tendulkar, when he was playing for Yorkshire, said he never really missed Indian food because there was so much of it in Leeds and Bradford.

After London, it is Birmingham and Bradford that are identified as the curry capitals of Britain. Although the restaurants here remain essential formula curry houses, no one is complaining. After all it's the taste that matters.

10

On the Curry Bus

What goes with chicken tikka masala, Britain's all-time favourite dish? The brewers would say beer – Indian beer – and the others would say basmati rice, naan and, of course, spices.

The curry industry brings along with it a large parallel industry. Indian brewers have been promoting Indian beers for a while now, saying that Indian beer is the only beer that goes with Indian food.

Bangalore-based Kingfisher (belonging to the United Breweries group) was the first to enter the UK market as early as 1982 when it was importing from India. In 1987 it began brewing under licence in Kent in partnership with Shepherd Neame. The beer is available in bottles and on draught in many Indian restaurants and marketing director Brian Dozey estimates that 6,500 Indian restaurants now sell the beer. Kingfisher won the gold medal in the premium lager class at the 2002 Brewing Industry International Awards. It is still the best-selling Indian lager brand. It sells in 330-ml, 500-ml and 660-ml bottles, and Kingfisher is one of the main sponsors of National Curry Day.

Kingfisher's cosy monopoly ended in 1990 when Cobra, another beer from Bangalore, was launched in the UK, followed up by an aggressive marketing campaign. Cambridge law graduate, Karan Bilimoria, was ready to give Kingfisher a run for its money.

It was the introduction of brewers of beer to Indian Army messes that gave Karan Bilimoria the idea to develop his own brand of Indian beer for the UK. Bilimoria next managed to persuade the Bangalore-based Mysore Brewery to develop his own style of beer especially for the export market.

In June 1990 Hindu priests in Bangalore blessed the beer and it arrived in Britain to be launched at a function at the Bombay Brasserie restaurant. Initially the beer was delivered door-to-door to Indian restaurants from a Citroen 2CV, but Cobra's aggressive marketing soon worked wonders. Cobra became the biggest-selling bottled Indian beer in the UK in less than six years. It also became one of the fastest-growing beer brands in the UK and in 1999 was listed as one of the top 100 companies in the *Sunday Times* Fast Track 100 League Table, for the fastest-growing companies in the UK.

In 1997, the beer moved from Bangalore to Bedford and Cobra began to be brewed in the Charles Wells brewery, the largest independent family-run brewery in the UK. Cobra is available in 330-ml and 660-ml bottles and on draught in some Indian restaurants. While Kingfisher remains the best-selling Indian beer on the market, Cobra sells the largest amount of bottled beer. Both are stocked by supermarkets like Waitrose, Tesco, Europa, Somerfield and Morrisons.

Cobra is now also available in Harrods and Selfridges and exports to twenty-three countries including Canada, Ireland, Belgium, Italy, Switzerland, Singapore, Italy and Russia.

Both beer companies mounted an aggressive nationwide advertisement campaign trying to corner the customers at the 8,500 Indian restaurants in Britain. Over October and November 1997, Kingfisher launched a major media campaign blitzing consumers in south-east England with the message that no Indian meal was complete without Kingfisher beer. Four hundred vibrantly coloured posters were put up at key tube and rail stations throughout London and the surrounding counties, hammering the message that Kingfisher was the beer to drink with vindaloo, tikka, tandoori and balti, all top-favourite Indian dishes.

Matching Kingfisher's colourful mega-campaign, Cobra stepped into the act in February 1998 with a Saatchi-designed campaign that had at its centre Dave, the self-confessed 'curryholic', who advises other curryholics that they can eat *more* curry if they drink Cobra, rather than other fizzy European lagers.

Over twelve months the nationwide 'curryholic' campaign focused on London, Birmingham, Manchester and Leeds, covering radio, press and outdoor advertising, as well as giant posters in London underground stations. One million cards were distributed, advertising the 'beer from Bangalore' and there was even a curryholic hotline number to contact.

The vast sums spent by both beer companies showed how high the stakes were in the beer industry in Indian restaurants. Both specifically targeted the Indian restaurant industry.

Much as upmarket Indian restaurants are trying to get away from the curry and lager image, the beer companies are out to enforce it. But the staggering facts are that 2.1 million pints of lager a week are consumed in Indian restaurants alone, which goes to show that there is no escaping the fact that most clients prefer beer with their curry. Paul Chichester-Constable of Team Saatchi said that beer drinkers in the UK are now choosing the brand according to the occasion, and therefore Cobra is advertising its authenticity as an Indian beer. 'Introducing "Dave" as a character gives us a chance to bring to life the concept of "curryholic" and introduce some fun into the brand. Eating curry can be fun and we want Cobra to reflect that.' Cobra even started a campaign to get the word 'curryholic' included in the Oxford English dictionary.

Other Indian beers in the market include Lal Toofan, and UB's Kalyani Export Special – 'the pride of Bengal' – which is available in 650-ml and 330-ml bottles imported from India. Kalyani beer is from Calcutta and is the biggest-selling lager brand in north India.

As already mentioned, the tradition of drinking Carlsberg with Indian food began with King

Gustav of Sweden. At the moment, Carlsberg remains the best-selling beer in Indian restaurants, commanding a 51 per cent share of all draught sales compared to Kingfisher's 23 per cent and Lal Toofan's 7 per cent.

Interestingly even in the late nineteenth and early twentieth century (*c.* 1890–1905), a few German companies were asked to open breweries in Mysore, and the beer had to be to the satisfaction of the Resident. Then as now, the beers most often thought to be appropriate for Indian food were from breweries in the same region, Mysore and Bangalore, and the beer preferred was European rather than dark and heavy English beers and ales.

In 1999 Karan Bilimoria also launched his own brand of wine, General Billy's (named after his father), to accompany Indian food. The four wines from the Languedoc region of France and three from the west coast of South Africa include Merlot, Sauvignon, Chardonnay and Shiraz. Between 1 November 1999 and 15 December 1999, Bilimoria sold around 2,500 bottles of General Billy's. General Billy's is stocked in many Indian restaurants now. Cobra beer now has a turnover approaching £50 million and Karan Bilimoria, known popularly as 'King Cobra', won the Asian of the Year Award in 2002.

Apart from Indian beers, there are many other accompaniments which come with Indian food. Basmati rice remains a big import, with several companies marketing the 'Rice from Dehradun and the Himalyan foothills'. There is a legend that fragrant basmati rice was brought to the Dehra Dun valley by Amir Dost Muhammad of Afghanistan when he was exiled there by the British in 1840.

The UK rice market is estimated to be worth over £160 million and includes varieties such as basmati, American white and brown long grain, easy cook, jasmine, risotto and wild rice. Britons apparently consume over 50,000 tons of rice each year (*Foodservice Intelligence*, June 2002).

The prince of rice is basmati, with Tilda, the brand leader, and Uncle Ben together accounting for 52 per cent of market share. Tilda advertises nationally on television and in the print media, and has captured the market over the last fifteen years. Behind the success of Tilda is low-profile businessman Rashmi Thakrar, fifty-six, popularly known as the 'Rice Boy'. Tilda rice is smartly packaged, slickly advertised and has a modern plant and private jetty in Essex. Uncle Ben is favoured by the catering sector.

Another popular brand is Veetee rice, with Indian-born Moni Varma giving tough competition to Thakrar. Veetee has an ultra-modern facility at Rochester in Kent, complete with its own jetty. Other basmati brands incude Guru, Dawat, Kiran, Natco, Vikas and East End Foods. Supermarkets like Sainsbury's and Tesco also stock their own brand of basmati rice available in 1-kg and 2-kg packs. The most popular size in the Tilda basmati rice range is the 20-kg bag, showing its high demand. In most cases the rice is aged and matured in warehouses in India and then transported to England where the companies mill it and package it in their rice mills.

Chapati flour, gram flour, daals and spices are just some of the other products needed to complete the ethnic kitchen, and wholesalers importing and selling these have made a fortune in Britain. The list of Asian millionaires in Britain include many names of those running cash-and-carry businesses, importing rice, wheat, daals and spices from the subcontinent and marketing them in the UK.

Sir Anwar Pervez and family are placed high on the list of Asian millionaires published by *Eastern Eye* newspaper and valued at around £155 million in 2001. The Pervez family came to Britain in the 1950s from Pakistan and Anwar worked as a bus conductor in Bradford before setting up the Bestway Cash and Carry business in 1976. The company is now a major force in wholesale food and has a turnover in excess of £1 billion. Anwar Pervez, a farmer's son, used to walk eight miles to school every day in Pakistan. His sons by contrast went to Eton, all of which goes to show that a little basmati and spices go a long way in Britain. In 1999 Perwez was knighted for his charitable efforts through the Bestway Foundation. Sir Anwar always organises a Charity Race Day at Ascot at which the Bestway marquee holds a charity auction.

Other Asian millionaires in the wholesale cash and carry business include Fakhruddin Suterwalla, sixty-three, who owns the TRS Cash and Carry business and is estimated to be worth £40 million, and Trilok Wouhra, a 65-year-old Sikh, who owns East End Foods in Birmingham, one of the major grocery businesses of the Midlands. He is valued at £16 million. And the most famous cash-and-carry millionaire is Mohammed Sarwar, owner of United Wholesale in Glasgow, who went on to become the first Muslim MP in the House of Commons in the May 1997 general election. Sarwar, a Labour MP, is worth £10 million. Bangladesh-born Iqbal Ahmed, forty-five, who set up Seafood Marketing International to import prawns, shrimps and other frozen fish from the Indian Ocean and the South China Sea, is estimated at £76 million and is one of the most successful Asian millionaires.

Recognising the potential of spice exports from India, as Indian food becomes a habit rather than an adventure in the West, the Spice Board of India has taken a keen initiative in promoting the trade. With total exports to the UK on the increase, the Spice Board organised a major Spice Food Festival in London in June 1998. It also participated in the Ethnic Food '98 Exhibition at Birmingham, displaying products from over thirty-five Indian companies.

The total export of spices from India equalled $450 million during 1999–2000. India accounts for 46 per cent of the world's spice exports. The bulk of the 10,000 tons plus of spices – including chillies, pepper, turmeric, ginger and curry powder – are purchased by private companies in the UK like TRS, BE International and McCormick who clean and repackage them for sale to local food companies. Christopher Columbus and Vasco da Gama may have begun the innings but the Spice Board of India is now definitely piling on the runs.

But the oldest of all Indian imports, and essentially the most popular in Britain, remains tea. Tea came to India from China. As early as 1689, John Ovington records that tea was taken by *banias* in Surat without sugar, or mixed with a small quantity of lemons, and sometimes with some spices.

The British began commercial tea planting in India in 1830, but the first plants brought from China did badly. It was Major Charles Bruce who reported that he had seen tea plants with thicker leaves growing in Assam and these, when planted, responded well. By 1864, £3 million worth of Indian tea was auctioned at London's Mincing Lane and in 1875 £26 million. Tea plantations sprang up all over Assam, the largest being the Assam Company of 1840 followed by several estates in Darjeeling (1853). Tea was also planted on the Nilgiri slopes and by 1839 tea was reported growing luxuriously in Nilgiri.

An article in the *Scientific American* as early as 1874 has a report on Indian tea which says:

The *Calcutta Gazette* informs us that efforts to extend the cultivation of the tea-plant in the northwest of India have been highly successful. The climate and soil in Kemaoon are as suited to the favourable growth of the shrub as the finest Chinese locality. Moreover, the tea-brokers in England have pronounced the India tea equal to China tea of a superior class, possessing the flavour of orange pekoe. The price at which tea can be raised is so low as to afford the greatest encouragement for the application of capital. The 100,000 acres available for tea cultivation in the Dhoon alone would yield 7,500,000 pounds, equal to one sixth of the entire consumption of England.

Today tea exports to Britain continue to grow and 27 million kg of Indian tea were imported into Britain in 1997. In the first six months of 1998 there was a 49 per cent rise in global exports. The Tea Board's export target for 2002 was 265 million kilograms.

The best place to sample Indian teas is Harrods, which stocks the largest range of Indian teas outside India. Harrods first opened as a tea merchant in 1849 and still sells the most exotic range of teas in the world. Harrods' Darjeeling teas include pure single-estate teas like Bloomfield GFOP (Golden Flower Orange Pekoe), a high quality light/medium tea from a famous estate, the Gielle GFOP, Makaibari GFOP, Margaret's Hope GFOP, Namring BOP (Broken Orange Pekoe), Risheehat GFOP and Seeyok GFOP, and Selimbong GFOP among others.

The Assam range includes Assam BOP, Greenwood GBOP (Golden Broken Orange Pekoe), Thowra GFOP, Keilung GBOP, Ghillidary GBOP and Doomni TGFOP (Tippy Golden Flower Orange Pekoe), a top-grade Assam tea that is rare and exquisite. In 2002 Harrods introduced eight new flavours of Assam tea in a special month-long promotion that included the colourful Bihu dancers from Assam performing in the Food Halls. The flavours included Baghjan Assam, Thowra Assam, Sessa Gold Assam, Mokalbari East Assam, Margherita Assam, Dejoo Mystique, Raj Garh Superfine and Orangajuli, all single-estate teas from the region.

Harrods also launched its own-label brand of Indian organic teas in July 1998. The growing demand for organic produce led Harrods to start researching into producing organic tea. To get a tea plantation to be certified as organic, it has to have the approval of Naturland, a member of the International Federation of Agriculture and inspected by the Institut of Marketecologie of Switzerland. The tea plantation has to operate in the organic method – by planting leguminous plants near tea bushes, and using herbal pesticides and natural fertilisers – for three years before it can get clearance.

Harrods is now growing organic tea in four gardens in India: the Selimbong garden at Pokhriabong, Darjeeling, which has won the Tea Board of India Award for quality; the Ambootia garden at Kurseong, Darjeeling; the Seeyok garden at Mirik, Darjeeling; and the Banaspatty garden at Karbi Anglong, Assam.

The tea is packed at a site adjacent to the tea gardens, to preserve maximum freshness. It is packed in simple brown handmade craft paper, recycled board, unbleached filter paper and natural jute fibre. The Harrods range of organic teas is priced from £5.25 to £9.75 per 125-gm chestlet.

Apart from Harrods, fine Indian teas can be found at Fortnum & Mason which has started selling a limited edition of First Flush Darjeeling teas, apart from its regular range of single-estate Assam and Darjeeling teas.

Twinings, the famous tea company that was started in 1706 by Thomas Twining, who set up as a tea merchant in the Strand, London, still stocks an exotic number of teas. The firm continues to trade from the same address, an amazing and unique record. Twinings offer a variety of loose vintage Darjeeling and Assam teas and also sells tea bags of the same. The shop in the Strand is a tea-lovers paradise where you are delighted by the fragrances of the various teas as you walk in.

Whittard of Chelsea also sells vintage Darjeeling Tippy Golden leaf tea, from Margaret Hope's estate among other single-estate teas. Jacksons of Piccadilly are the other big tea merchants in the UK, packaging and selling vintage Darjeeling and Assam teas in attractive boxes and gift sets. All the supermarkets do their own brands of Darjeeling and Assam teas. Ever since the Indian Tea Board started to stamp the teas with its own certificate of authenticity, it has become easy to identify authentic Assam and Darjeeling teas and distinguish them from the fake and blended Darjeeling and Assam teas in the market.

The cup that cheers from India has done well in Britain, selling more than canned drinks, soft drinks and even lager. And the whole industry surrounding Indian food, from beers to basmatis, has successfully climbed on to the curry bandwagon, doing remarkably well for themselves.

11

Conclusion

So what are we to make of the curry craze, of the cuisine that changed the eating habits of a nation, and threw up curry houses up and down the country from remote Scottish islands to bustling London and small coastal villages in the south? How do we assess the cuisine that created millionaires, that survived a recession, the market fallout of 11 September 2001, and that is evolving every day? Well, the future is definitely bright for all those involved in the Indian food business. All those supplying ready-made food to supermarkets and retail outlets are looking at expansion. Those in the pub trade and café trade have all started branches and nearly all are considering a chain of franchised cafés or pubs. Slowly but steadily Indian food chains are becoming a reality, as much as American fast-food joints, and British restaurant/café chains.

Big money is more ready to enter the Indian food business now than ever before. Roger Myers, founder of the Café Rouge chain and present head of Punch Taverns, is planning to pump £40 million into a chain of balti pubs in partnership with Pele

(Parminder Bains). Cyrus Todiwala of the Café Spice Namaste has been backed by Michael Gottlieb, ex-chairman of the Restaurateurs Association of Great Britain (RAGB) and owner of the upmarket themed restaurant Smollensky's on the Strand. He also has backing from Martin Jacque, Gottlieb's partner at Smollensky's. Other shareholders include the McCarthy group, closely associated with Richard Branson. La Porte des Indes opened in London as a branch of the international Blue Elephant Group. It goes to show that financiers are realising that there are profits to be made by backing the Indian food/restaurant industry.

One of the first calls G.K. Noon received after his factory burnt down was from David Sainsbury, head of Sainsbury's, who was ready to help him out of the crisis with a major financial backing. Indian chilled food at Sainsbury's is big business and the supermarket did not want their chief supplier to pack up.

Chilled curries from supermarkets are probably the biggest profit-makers in the curry crusade. Britain has been dubbed the 'King of Ping cuisine', or the biggest consumers of microwave heatable pre-cooked meals. A survey by Mintel, the marketing company, in 2003 revealed that sales of chilled dishes had increased by 90 per cent in the past four years. The market itself is worth £2 billion a year. Compared to the Continent, British housewives have shown their preference for abandoning their pots and pans in favour of ready-made 'Ping cuisine', so named after the ping sound the microwave makes to tell you the food is ready. The amount spent by Britons on ready meals is twice as much as the French and Germans, four times as much as the Italians and six times as much as the Spanish.

More than three-quarters of British housewives regularly serve up ready meals as compared with only a third of Italians. At least one in three Britons eats at least one such meal a week, twice the consumption in France.

And of course, leading the chilled food ready-meal range is the curry. Tesco, Britain's biggest supermarket chain, says its chicken tikka masala and rice meal is the third highest selling meal in the store. Marks & Spencer confirms similarly that its chicken tikka masala is the fourth highest seller in the store after lasagne and chicken kiev.

It is good news for curry manufacturers like G.K. Noon and Perween Warsi who are all expanding their outlets and building more factories. It is good news for labour as the new factories create more jobs at a time when the global economy is on a slow-down.

But what of the restaurants and the curry houses that started the whole revolution? 'I think the future is bleak for curry houses,' said Iqbal Wahhab, founder of the Cinnamon Club. 'I think that they will become the victims of their own success and will be wiped out by the super-markets. The supermarkets offer cheap food and of consistent quality. They are the biggest com-petition for the curry houses.'

Wahhab feels that the standard Bangladeshi-run curry houses will become a dying institution in the next years if they do not either improve dramatically or try to keep up with the competition:

> They are all family-run institutions. In the past, if somebody's uncle was running a restaurant, they would go up and ask for a job. If they were good looking they would be hired as waiters, if not they would be sent to the kitchen, that's how it worked. But things are changing now. The second generation doesn't want to work the long hours and that will be a major problem for these curry houses. They will run out of staff.

Although the government has now relaxed immigration laws for chefs from three-year to five-year permits, there are still curry houses around the country waiting up to a year to get a suitable chef. Many skilled Indian chefs may be illiterate, and therefore would not pass the legal requirements for entry into Britain, creating further problems. Their skill would have been passed down from generations but they couldn't get past the immigration procedures. Under the circumstances, most curry houses simply rely on family members to help out in the kitchen.

While upmarket Indian restaurants import chefs from the subcontinent, usually headhunting them from India's five-star hotels like the Oberoi or the Taj group, the middle-level restaurants and the curry houses have problems sourcing their chefs. They are affected if there is a delay due to immigration procedures.

Sherin Alexander of La Porte des Indes says it isn't just chefs who are difficult to find, but the total lack of skilled waiting staff and front-of-house staff:

It is very difficult to get trained waiters, trained front-of-house staff. There are very few Asian women who want to come forward in the restaurant business. I would like to see more women staff, in lovely saris, in my restaurant. But I just can't get them. They do not go into the industry, for whatever stigma it has. They'll work in shops, at tills, but they won't work in restaurants.

The Home Office has announced funds to set up establishments to teach local staff how to cook Indian food. But it seems highly unlikely that young second-generation Asian school and college leavers will be enthusiastic enough to go to chef-training schools. Most have earmarked a different career for themselves as professionals, since being a chef requires long and anti-social working hours.

In June 1998 the Department of Education came up with a grant of £300,000 for an Asian Academy of Culinary Skills, based at the Thames Valley University near Southall. The headlines in the daily papers were immediately sneering. The *Daily Mail* described it as the University of Madras, the *Daily Telegraph* as Vindaloo Academy. The headlines reflected that the British were ready to eat their curry every day, but not prepared to take it seriously.

Andrew Ward, head of corporate relations at Thames Valley University, travelled to Delhi to study the upmarket cafés and bars that have sprung up there in recent years. What the university would like to do is to train its students in the whole package of Indian food, taking it away from the flock-wallpaper curry house image. 'At the moment, it's where people go after the pub,' said Ward.

To the owners of small and medium-sized restaurants, the university course is probably making the best out of a bad situation. They lack the clout of a top restaurant like the Bombay Brasserie, which can rely on its trained Taj chefs from India, and the legal paperwork involved in getting a chef from India is even more cumbersome for these small businesses.

Asif Rahman, of the Lahore Karahi restaurant in Southall, is actively interested in the training project. He bemoans the fact that chefs in this country routinely use ready-made pastes to cook their meals. He is also keen to train them to improve their image and wants a modern look to the old curry houses – no flock wallpaper, no tablecloths, chefs working in an open-plan area, and a deli-style counter displaying raw spices and homemade sweets.

The academy wants to provide training for front-of-house staff and courses in marketing and design. 'We want to encourage young Asians to get out of the ghetto, to turn professional, and take the Indian restaurant industry upmarket.'

Most curry houses still pay their employees a pittance, and most are staffed by Bangladeshi students who are working part-time. Securing skilled staff, who will command better pay and reflect a more professional upmarket restaurant, is what the Academy has in mind. The course has become very popular, and many Asians are now entering the Academy to spruce up their skills. In the 2002 academic year, 43 Asians enrolled, and they all passed.

Cyrus Todiwala is actively involved in training programmes and frequently goes to colleges to give talks on Indian food, and train cooks. 'Training is a must, we need proper skilled staff, otherwise the industry won't survive,' he says.

Also hot on the training circuit is the chef-proprietor of Rasa, the famous Kerala vegetarian restaurant that has won rave reviews ever since it started. Das Sreedharan, a passionate cook and a real stickler for authenticity (all his recipes are personally learnt from his mum and his cuisine is exclusively that of the Nairs of Kerala), is actively involved in training and is going to be one of the teachers at the Thames Valley University:

We have to teach people how to cook these authentic dishes, or they will die out. Half the food that is served here is not Indian food at all, it is all from bottles and jars. I believe in grinding the spices every day. There are no short cuts.

Whether the vindaloo schools will turn out authentic curries remains to be seen. But at any rate, the restaurant industry is out to modernise and improve. They realise they have the people hooked, the task before them is now to refine the taste.

At the moment the restaurant industry has a turnover of £2 billion a year – something that cannot be ignored. Add to this the turnovers from those in the food manufacturing business, from supermarkets, and from curry paste manufacturers and one can see the huge potential in the field.

London has seen a profusion of upmarket Indian restaurants in the past few years [says Sherin Alexander]. I think it's reached saturation point at the moment. Each restaurant is trying to do something different, has its own vibrancy, is using top PR companies to draw in the glamorous crowds. It's good for the image of Indian restaurants, it's good competition which keeps everyone on their toes.

But no matter how upmarket or how chic they become, many Indian restaurants feel they are never considered in the same class as the top European restaurants. 'The French restaurants are always up there, and the Indian down there,' said Samar Hamid of Café Lazeez. 'People don't mind paying a price in a French restaurant but they grumble if they have to pay at an Indian restaurant. It's just an image problem.' Namita Panjabi, who runs two successful upmarket restaurants in London, agrees that Indian restaurants, despite offering the ambience and the gourmet cuisine, have to price themselves lower than French restaurants.

Indian restaurants are still seen as something being started and run by immigrant unemployed Bangladeshis serving cheap food. No one, it seems, wants to pay anything above average at an Indian restaurant, never mind the service and ambience.

The reason could well be found in the colonial history of the two countries. When the British first came to India, the common soldiers, the single Englishmen and the first travellers all enjoyed Indian food. After the Mutiny, things native were shunned with a vengeance and the emphasis was to go European again. Company officials who wore Indian dress, had Indian friends and enjoyed Indian food and customs were subject to ridicule. If they persisted, they were quickly and quietly retired and replaced by a new breed of English public-school-educated officials who despised mixing the races. But the overriding popularity of Indian food could not be ignored, and fusion food was already developing between the two communities. Food, like other Indian things, became grounds for a class divide.

While the lower and middle classes would frankly confess to enjoying Indian foods, the aristocracy would look down on it. The rulers would inevitably have to insist on the superiority of all things European and the dumbing down in the process of all things Indian, from music to medicine and food, none of which were ever acknowledged as being anything more than pedestrian.

In *Culinary Jottings from Madras* by 'Wyvern' (real name Colonel Kenney-Herbert) this fact is recognised:

> While it cannot be denied that the banishment of curries from our high art banquet is necessary, there can be no doubt that at mess and club dinners, at hotels and at private houses, these time-honoured dishes will always be welcome.

'Wyvern' was among those who was so attached to Indian cuisine that he set up a cookery school in England after he retired from the Raj.

Even the *grande dame* of nineteenth-century cookery writers, Isabella Beeton, whose mighty tome *Mrs Beeton's Book of Household Management* (1861) was the bible for British women, wrote about Indian food without ever having visited India. Though her tone was usually disparaging, creating the impression that the memsahib was sure to be cheated by the natives, even Mrs Beeton could not afford to ignore Indian food. On the famous curry powder she wrote: 'Some persons prefer to make it at home, but that purchased at any respectable shop is generally speaking far superior.' Mrs Beeton herself had some fourteen different recipes for curry powder in her book.

The inclination to shun Indian food was very much part of the Raj psyche, but the popularity of it at one-to-one level between the Indians and the English could not be discounted. While all the other influences of the Raj travelled from west to east – cricket, tea, education, parliament and the legal system – the only Indian influence that made a lasting impression on the British was Indian food.

But the snobbery of the establishment succeeded in keeping it out of the élite club. It is only today that upmarket Indian restaurants are drawing in the trendy crowds – the rockers and socialites – and the Indian restaurant is becoming a fashion statement. As Indian things like *mehendi* (henna), bindis, salwars, yoga and meditation are becoming a fad in the West, adopted by the likes of Madonna, Kate Winslett and Jemima Khan, the stunningly decorated spicy interiors of the upmarket cafés and brasseries are also coming into their own. Noticeably they are shedding their old Raj and colonial hangover, celebrating the Indian spirit and staking their claim to be at the top end of London's haute cuisine. 'If a French chef can get away with £55 a head just for the food, and £95 with drinks, why can't we?' said Cyrus Todiwala of Café Spice Namaste. 'Our food is more intricate, more complicated and more difficult to prepare. It's all about perception.'

But even though the upmarket restaurants today are moaning, they cannot blame the Bangladeshis – who started the curry-house routine – for creating the cheap and cheerful image:

It is they who laid the foundation of this business. They are the ones who took it all over the country. Today we are here because of them [said Cyrus Todiwala]. Eighty per cent of Indian restaurants in the country are still owned and run by Bangladeshis. They cooked their way into the English hearts, and everything else is because of them.

Again it was the Bangladeshi restaurateurs that bore the brunt of racism in the early years and still carried on plying their trade. As lager louts came in for their Friday night beer and curry, there were inevitably instances of racial insult and abuse. This continues in curry houses today which attract the late-night curry and lager louts. A group of drunken yobs, dropping in after the pubs to sweat over a steamy vindaloo, is unfortunately one of the tarnished images of the high-street curry house.

Michelin star chef, Vineet Bhatia, agrees that without the Bangladeshi curry houses, he would not have been here. At Zaika he employs some Bangladeshi waiters who are given proper training:

I am here because of what they started. They faced the racism and insults and made the cuisine popular. They did what they could do then. I believe it is for Indian restaurants like us to take the cuisine further and bring in the true flavours of India.

Bhatia says he has no problem charging £60 and more per head for meals at Zaika and finds that people are prepared to pay for quality and ambience.

Today even the routine high street curry house is seriously considering an image revamp. A walk down Brick Lane in east London, home to a large Bangladeshi population, and previously a run-down and shabby area, now reveals a street full of trendy bars, cafés and fashion shops. It is even trying to promote itself as Bangla Town. It reflects the mood of the high street curry house which wants to be part of London's fashion statement. Café Naz on Brick Lane, with its contemporary furniture, cool lighting and café atmosphere, is just one example of the new-look Bangladeshi restaurant which can hardly be recognised as a curry house any more.

The food on offer is changing as well. More and more Bangladeshi restaurants are turning towards serving authentic Bengali food – fish curries, rezala, etc. Indian restaurants at the same time are going in for regional cuisine. All agree that the market is turning more discerning and both the menu and the service have to be of a higher standard.

And as the restaurants serve regional dishes, the supermarkets follow them closely. Waitrose,

Sainsbury's and Marks & Spencer have a range of regional cuisine offering flavours of India from the Malabar coast to eastern India and Andhra Pradesh.

A Mintel survey back in 1994 found that the ethnic food market was becoming more and more exotic as customers were not happy with standard curries alone. The survey found that:

- a growth of 17 per cent was expected in the ethnic foods in the retail sector
- the market was worth £370 million
- Indian food sales increased 80 per cent between 1989 and 1993
- poppadoms alone were worth £8.5 million.

Two years later in 1996, a Patak's survey found that the retail Indian food market had grown to £750 million – doubled in two years – as more and more English people cooked Indian food in their own homes.

In 1996 Cobra carried out a survey at the BBC Good Food Show in London and found:

- 68 per cent of the public visit an Indian restaurant at least once a month
- each person spends an average of £17.93 when they visit an Indian restaurant
- 75 per cent of people cook an Indian meal at home at least once a month
- 40 per cent of people eat a ready-made Indian meal at least once a month

- 67 per cent of people prefer an Indian restaurant, five times more than Chinese.

At the beginning of the twenty-first century, Indian restaurants (estimated at around 8,500) far outnumber Chinese restaurants, which number around 5,000. Britons eat 200 million poppadoms and 50,000 tons of rice a year. The industry has an annual turnover of £2.4 billion and employs 56,000 workers.

Whether it is 'ping cuisine' or people eating at Indian restaurants, the taste for Indian food is evolving and still rising. Indian restaurants have finally broken the Michelin barrier and have made the grade among the other coveted London restaurants. There is hope for more stars in the future as Indian restaurants push out the boat to get the coveted recognition from the Michelin man.

The news is good for those churning out chicken kormas and ready-made sauces from their factory floors. It is optimistic for those with chic and trendy cafés, pubs and restaurants, who are putting an exploding variety of regional Indian cooking on the restaurant scene. Cheap air fares mean more people are taking exotic holidays in Goa and Kerala and Rajasthan and demanding the food when they get back. Restaurants and supermarkets are all flush with regional cuisine which is the new way forward.

And what of the standard curry house? What lies in store for the Last Days of the Raj and The Royal

Bengal Tandoori. Well, they brought about the revolution; they are not ready to die yet. After all, what is the best known curry-house invention – chicken tikka masala – remains Britain's Number One dish even today. Marks & Spencer alone sells a packet of chicken tikka masala every four seconds a branch is open. And no amount of smart Kerala, Hyderabadi or Bengali cooking has managed to displace that.

Again, it was a takeaway from Bradford, not a fancy delivery from Conran's Le Pont de Tour or Bluebird, that Princess Diana, Mick Jagger, Liz Hurley, Elle Macpherson, Susannah Constantine and a host of other London jetsetters tucked into when Imran and Jemima Khan threw a fundraising charity dinner at the Dorchester to raise money for his cancer hospital. Princess Diana wore a salwar kameez, the event received endless media coverage and the food came from the Nawaab restaurant in Bradford, a place completely unknown to the Michelin man. It was the first time such a thing had happened at the Dorchester. Needless to say everyone had a wonderful time.

Anyone fancy a curry?

Restaurants: a select guide

Key: £ Under £20 per head
    £££ £20–£35 per head
    £££ Over £35 per head

SPECIALIST INDIAN RESTAURANTS

Bengal Clipper
££

Cardamom Building
Shad Thames
Butler's Wharf
London
SE1 2YR
Tel: 0207 357 9001

The biggest plus point for this restaurant is the location, minutes from Tower Bridge, on the historic Spice Wharf with its colourful shops and restaurants. The downside is that the restaurant doesn't actually have the river view (Conran got there first).

Still historically the best site to serve up the cuisine of Bengal at a location where the clipper ships from Bengal sailed up the Thames and unloaded their spices. The elegantly decorated restaurant is very much about celebrating Bengali cuisine – serving such specialities as golda chingri (a giant prawn from the Bay of Bengal), Bengal tiger fish hara masala (green fish curry), shorshay bata golda chingri (giant prawns in mustard paste), sathkari gosht (lamb cooked in wild lemon and fiery naga chillies) and a selection of Bengali-style spinach using seasonal spinach from Bangladesh. The chef incidentally won the Spinach Master Chef Award and the range of spinach is definitely worth trying. Also a range of Goan dishes like haas vindaloo (duck vindaloo). Most dishes are fairly hot.

Branch

Bengal Trader	Liverpool St
	1 Parliament Court
	Artillery Lane
	Spitalfields, London
	E1 7NA
	Tel: 0207 375 0072

Bobbys	154–6 Belgrave Road
£	Leicester
	LE4 5AT
	0116 266 0106

Vegetarian restaurant in the heart of Leicester's Asian shopping mall with sari shops and jewellery stores on both sides. Pakoras, chaat, paneer shashlik, and a popular thali.

Bombay Brasserie	Courtfield Close
£££	Courtfield Road
	London
	SW7 4UH
	Tel: 0207 370 4040

The theme is very much 'last days of the Raj', with a cool neo-colonial ambience. This restaurant has consistently maintained its standard some twenty years on. High point is the crescent-shaped conservatory. Very busy in the evenings so booking is a must, especially if you want to sit in the conservatory. Sunday buffet very popular. Good selection of north Indian, Goan and Parsi cuisine. Take your pick from starters like shrimp bezule (crispy fried shrimps tossed with mustard seeds, curry leaves and green chillies) and crab pattice. Parsi specialities like chilli pomfret and house specialities like lamb nehari (lamb shanks cooked in gravy), lamb chettinad and fish malabar (sea bass cooked in coconut milk).

Britannia Spice 150 Commercial Street
££ Edinburgh Leith
EH6 6LB
Tel: 0131 555 2255

In a tourist hot-spot near the Royal Yacht *Britannia*, the Britannia Spice continues the nautical theme in the interior with an upper deck and a lower deck. There are timber floors and a sailcloth all adding to the liner experience. The menu is an eclectic mix of north Indian, Bangladeshi, Sri Lankan and Thai. Specialities include machcher bhorta (baked fish) starters, and shotkari ghost (lamb cooked in a fragrant juice with lemon leaves and Bengal chillies) and amer murgh (chicken cooked in mango pulp and cream).

Café Lazeez 88 St John Street
££ London
EC1M 4EH
Tel: 0207 253 2244

Chrome and glass metallic minimalist-style café with an open kitchen and a conservatory in a listed building in the city area. Very chic and European with a variety of traditional Indian and Indo-European fusion cooking. Low on fat and fire content. A traditional menu and an evolved menu for those who like a bit of fusion. Specialities include starters like salmon tikka and sesame fried wings and main course includes yoghurt tilapia, nalli gosht (lamb on the bone) and chilli chicken masala. The evolved menu offers cumin crusted sea bass and pistachio lamb.

Branches
Café Lazeez   93–5 Old Brompton Road
London
SW7 3LD
Tel: 0207 581 9993

This one has live jazz in the evening.

Café Lazeez   21 Dean Street
Soho
London
W1V 5AH
Tel: 0207 434 9393

Standard poor at the bar/brasserie upstairs, with terrible toilets to be shared with the Soho Theatre. Even the glass-top tables were crusty and dirty. All right, it's Soho, but so what?

Café Lazeez   116 Wharfside Street
The Mailbox
Birmingham
BR1 1RF
Tel: 0121 643 7979

Definitely worth a visit. Fabulous location and decor; excellent food and service.

Café Spice Namaste　　　　　　16 Prescott Street
££　　　　　　　　　　　　　　　　London
　　　　　　　　　　　　　　　　　E1 8AZ
　　　　　　　　　　　　Tel: 0207 488 9242

Vibrant decor, warm colours and cheerful staff. Cyrus Todiwala's exciting menu includes masala nu roast gos (parsee roast lamb), beef xacutti, vindalho de porco (pork vindaloo), dhanajeera ni seabass (sea bass with cumin and coriander seeds), wild boar sausages, piri piri chicken tikka and dhansak. Exotic meats on the speciality menu include ostrich, venison, pheasant and kangaroo. All cooked Indian-style, mostly as tikkas or kebabs or in a masala curry. Full at lunchtime with city clientele. Evenings quieter. Closed on Sundays.

Branch
Café Spice Namaste　　　　　　247 Lavender Hill
　　　　　　　　　　　　　　　　Battersea
　　　　　　　　　　　　　　　　　London
　　　　　　　　　　　　　　　　　SW11
　　　　　　　　　　　　Tel: 0207 738 1717

Same lavish decor and exciting menu. Buzzing in the evenings. Open every day.

Chor Bizarre　　　　　　　　16 Albemarle Street
££　　　　　　　　　　　　　　　　Mayfair
　　　　　　　　　　　　　　　　　London
　　　　　　　　　　　　　　　　　W1X 3HA
　　　　　　　　　　　　Tel: 0207 629 8542

Deliberate pun on 'bazar' gives restaurant its quirky name. Based on the 'Chor Bazar' concept from India. Literally a thieves' den in Mayfair filled with furniture, paintings and artefacts bought from all the chor bazaars of Delhi, Calcutta and Bombay. Flush with antiques, lamps, chairs and jewellery. Even a four-poster bed from Calcutta converted into a table. No two things match and everything is arranged like a den. Keeps you busy looking around. If there's something you fancy, it's for sale! Booking essential especially if you are a big group, because it is small and can get filled quickly. Menu includes Kashmiri specialities like mirchi korma and goshtaba and haaq (spinach cooked in a Kashmiri style).

Branch
Chor Bizarre   4/15 A Asaf Ali Road
                                                     New Delhi 110002
                                                     Tel: 91 11 2327 3821

Chutney Mary   535 Kings Road
£££   London
                                                            SW10 0SZ
                                                   Tel: 0207 351 3113

Fashionable Chelsea restaurant that has just enjoyed a total revamp. Original Anglo-Indian theme and Raj appeal has been done away with to make it more contemporary and modern. Emphasis is now on regional cooking with chefs from Goa, Kerala, Hyderabad, Lucknow, Delhi and Bombay serving up the exciting menu. Starters include an exotic selection of crab claws with pepper and garlic, nahari lamb soup, quail seekh kebabs, oysters served Goan style and Cochin-style squid. Main courses include some unusual dishes like tandoori partridge and guinea fowl almond korma, and some traditional regional favourites like Mangalore prawns and masala lamb shank shakuti.

Closed weekdays at lunchtime.

Cinnamon Club
££

The Old Westminster Library
Great Smith Street
London
SW1P 3BU
Tel: 0207 222 2555

Elegant decor throughout and a fabulous location at The Old Westminster Library, a Grade II listed building. The original look of the library has been retained with book-lined shelves and a gallery. No poppadoms here as Iqbal Wahhab's dream project has no place for them. A varied menu with some traditional Indian regional dishes and others with a European twist. Lunch menu is changed every week. Choose from starters like tandoor seared tuna and chilli fried squid with squid ink naan, and main courses that range from traditional Hyderabadi birianis and roast lamb saddle with green chilli and yoghurt to Rajasthani roast venison and pan-seared black cod. A side dish of Rajasthani sangri beans was a discovery (head chef Vivek Singh is after all from Rajasthan and has some exciting recipes from there up his sleeve).

The all-day bar is popular and serves cocktails like lychee bellini and mango martini.

The restaurant is also open for breakfast and serves a range from dosas to stuffed parathas and salmon kedgeree to a traditional English fry-up. Expect to bump into politicians.

Eye of the Tiger
££

207 Old Christchurch Road
Bournemouth
Dorset
BH1 1JZ
Tel: 01202 317508

An innovative menu in this Bangladeshi/Indian restaurant with many of the dishes cooked with cointreau, tia maria or drambuie. Take your pick from tandoori quail, and tandoori trout, or duck breast tandoori, or prawn tikka and chicken tikka balti.

La Porte des Indes 32 Bryanston Street
£££ London
W1H 7AE
Tel: 0207 224 0055

If you like an opulent setting, this has it all: a waterfall, a marble staircase and exotic palms. Enough space on both floors (the restaurant seats about 320) to allow for an unhurried relaxed dinner. Exciting menu and convenient location, minutes from Marble Arch. Do go to the basement Jungle Bar where the floor is covered with peanut shells. Owner Sherin expects you to simply chuck your peanut shells on the floor. You'll love it once you get over your squeamishness. Wonderful cocktails including a tender coconut with rum and vanilla called Pondicherry mon cheri. Indo-French cuisine on offer from Pondicherry, Mahe and Karikal, the old French colonies. Other regional specialities also available. Staff are only too willing to guide you through the menu if the French names look a little too much. Try the Pondicherry recipes – policha meen (mullet marinated with green pepper, garlic and shallots and wrapped in a banana leaf and grilled). There is also the magret de cunard pulivar (duck breasts cooked in exotic spices), chumudu karaikal (sliced beef stir-fried with onion and whole roasted spices from the Christian community of Karaikal). Recommended starters are stir-fried squid with pepper and garlic and crab malabar.

Masala Zone   9 Marshall Street
£   London
                                                    W1F 7ER
                                          Tel: 0207 287 9966

Another superb venture from Namita Panjabi and sister
Camellia Panjabi. Good Indian food at cheap prices in
bright café setting. The Wagamama of Indian fast food and
street food. With the Warli tribal paintings on the wall and
the open kitchen, the place is ideal for shoppers on Oxford
Street. Excellent value thalis, curried noodles and chaats.
    Even an Ayurvedic thali for the health-conscious or the
diabetic.

Mela   152–6 Shaftesbury Avenue
£   London
                                                    WC2H 8HL
                                          Tel: 0207 836 8635

Where can you eat a good meal for under a fiver in the West
End at lunch time? The answer is of course Mela, with its
popular Paratha Pavilion started by Kuldip Singh, formerly
head chef at Soho Spice. The country-style cuisine in Mela
deliberately creates the dhaba atmosphere with an open
kitchen and a variety of tandoor and tava dishes, re-creating
the sort of food you get in street stalls in India. Bright warm
interiors with photographs of rural fairs and festivals.
    A serving of sarson ka saag (mustard spinach) and makki
ki roti (maize paratha), a north Indian speciality was priced
unbelievably at £1.95! And delicious it was too, without
being over-oily, as parathas tend to get. Singh must have
done his calculations for the place is always buzzing,
morning and evenings. The Paratha Pavilion (inspired by
Old Delhi's Parathey Wali Gali) is highly recommended for
lunchtime (price £4.95 for a paratha and curry). Other

specialities on the menu are the achari murg tikka, burra champ madiri (cuts of lamb, marinated in rum and spices overnight and cooked over charcoal) and tawe ke bathak (breast of duck, pot roasted with coconut, coriander, cumin and flavoured with mint and coriander). Also traditional Bengali fish curry and Allepy fish curry from Kerala.

Much favoured by *Bombay Dreams* composer, A.R. Rahman, director Shekhar Kapur, and director Ismail Merchant, who have studios in the area and often drop in for a bite.

Winner of the Carlton Best Indian Restaurant of the Year for 2001.

Branch: from the Mela group

Chowki	2–3 Denman Street
	London
	W1D 7HA
	Tel: 0207 836 8635

Mr Singhs	149 Elderslie Street
££	Glasgow
	Tel: 0141 204 0186

Very much a Punjab-comes-to-Scotland feel about this popular restaurant. Waiters here wear kilts and waitresses wear salwar kameezes. Haggis pakoras are a speciality, as are a number of fusion dishes like orange and chilli poussin in hoisin sauce with lemon grass fried rice, and chargrilled swordfish sprinkled with herbs. Traditional Indian as well with dosas and aloo tikki.

Quilon   41 Buckingham Gate
£££   London
                                       SW1E 6AF
                              Tel: 0207 821 1899

Sister restaurant of the Bombay Brasserie and owned by
the Taj group. Delicious coastal cuisine mainly from
Kerala. Winner of the *Good Curry Guide 2001* Best UK
Indian Restaurant. Impeccable decor, service and menu.
Take your pick from pepper shrimps, grilled scallops,
chicken chilli fry, Cochin mixed seafood broth, mussels
mappas (mussels cooked with onion, ginger, curry leaves
and turmeric powder and coriander poweder), red snapper
reshad (red snapper marinated and crispy fried),
chargrilled sea bass, and Allepy fish curry (fish cubes
cooked in red chilli and raw mango), lamb green curry and
Mangalore chicken curry.

Rasa   6 Dering Street
££   London
                                        W1R 9AB
                              Tel: 0207 629 1346

Kerala cuisine has never been more popular. This one is
for the dedicated veggie looking for something different.
The restaurant was one of the first in London to offer
speciality Kerala cuisine. All recipes belong exclusively to
the Nair community of Kerala and were personally taught
to owner Das Sreedharan by his mother. All chefs are from
the Nair community. Sreedharan serves a selection of pre-
meal snacks like achappam, pappadavadai, chinnapam,
pappadom, and chena upperi (a selection of papads, and
tea snacks available in Kerala's street-side tea shops).
Soups include rasam, parippu (a lentil soup) and
muringakol soup (drumsticks in tamarind water).

Main courses include such specialities as kadachakka stew (aubergine stew cooked in coconut milk), ulli theeya (red shallots cooked in coconut milk), veluthulli curry (garlic, cloves and shallots simmered in tamarind and curry leaves) and vendaka cheera kozhambu (spinach and okra stir-fried with shallots, red chillies and garlic). A variety of rice – tamarind rice, lemon rice, thakkali choru (rice cooked in coconut milk) – is also available.

This branch has now started a non-vegetarian section upstairs and serves a north Kerala menu from the Muslim families of Kerala.

Branches

Rasa
55 Church Street
Stoke Newington
London
N16 0AR
Tel: 0207 249 0344

Rasa Samudra
5 Charlotte Street
London
W1P 1HD
Tel: 0207 637 0222

Kerala fish restaurant with exotic fish preparations from the region.

Rasa Travancore
56 Church Street
Stoke Newington
London
N16 0NB
Tel: 0207 249 1340

Rasa Express

327 Euston Road
London
NW1 3AD
Tel:

Kerala fast-food restaurant that serves light and healthy lunchtime snacks to take away or eat in.

Red Fort
£££

77 Dean Street
London
W1D 3SH
Tel: 0207 437 2525

The newly revamped Red Fort has been given a fresh lease of life with an elegant decor and a new menu. With its red sandstone imported Jaipur stone and water feature, the restaurant looks fresh and contemporary. Food here retains its authentic Mughal dum pukht quality. For starters choose from galauti kebabs and monkfish tikkas. Main courses include specialities like anaari champ, and tandoori pasliaan (rack of lamb with black pepper and cumin sauce). Avadhi gosht biriani is a speciality as are traditional dishes like murgh mirchi ka salan.

Check out Bar Akbar in the basement, which was voted 'Bar of the week' by the *Sunday Telegraph*. Bar snacks like fish Amritsari and goolar kebab, all reasonably priced around £5 per plate.

Shimla Pinks
££

214 Broad Street
Birmingham
B15 1AY
Tel: 0121 633 0366

Bollywood meets Birmingham in this restaurant lavishly decorated with pink and wood with a dance club attached. A place, as its name suggests, for the bright young things of India to party and dine in. The £1.2 million refurbishment in 2002 brought the restaurant up to date with some of the upmarket Indian restaurants in Britain, bringing celebrities like David Ginola and Nick Owen to the restaurant.

Specialities are the gourmet buffet offering a variety of murgh malai tikka, lamb kebabs, lamb karahi, chicken tikka masala, Amritsari fish and mushroom shashlik.

Branch
Shimla Pinks   65–9 London Road
                                             Leicester
                                             LE2 OPE
                                             Tel: 0116 247 1471

Soho Spice   124–6 Wardour Street
££   Soho
                                             London
                                             W1V 3LA
                                             Tel: 0207 434 0808

This was the restaurant that started the trend of brightly designed Indian cafés offering food at reasonable prices in the heart of the West End. Amin Ali's all-day café with its vivid interiors, waiters in brightly dressed khadi kurtas, always had a feel-good atmosphere. The Hindi music in the background is all part of the ethnic chic, but the food is good and the price reasonable. Achari murg tikka and seekh kebabs make good starters. Main courses include hare murgh ka tikka, adrak ke panje (lamb chops marinated in ginger and spices), Malabar seafood korma and avial (a south Indian vegetable speciality). Or simply go for the mixed tandoori platter which has an excellent selection. Very packed on weekends as the queues build up for both the restaurant and the buzzing bar downstairs.

Once we queued for over an hour to get in! Can get noisy, but the place to go to for the buzz of Soho.

Suruchi
££

14a Nicolson Street
(opposite Festival Theatre)
Edinburgh
EH8 9DH
Tel: 0131 556 6583

Owned by photographer Herman Rodrigues and his wife Aabha, the restaurant has constantly been voted among the top Indian restaurants in Edinburgh. It was awarded the Best Indian Restaurant in Scotland in 1996 and travel writer William Dalrymple describes it as such. With chefs imported from India, the Rodrigues have done their best to bring the true flavour of India to their restaurant. Menu includes a variety of dishes from north and south India including lamb tikka and kebabs, chicken massalam, lamb shakuti, and even haggis pakoras as a Scottish Indian experience.

Branch
Suruchi

121 Constitution Street
Leith
Edinburgh
EH6 7AE
Tel: 0131 554 3268

Tamarind
£££

20 Queen Street
Mayfair
London
W1J 5PR
Tel: 0207 629 3561

Michelin-starred Mayfair restaurant offering excellent service, good food and a stylish, elegant decor with a view of the kitchen. Chef Alfred Prasad makes a mean lamb chop with crushed black pepper. The adraki jhinga (king prawns marinated in yoghurt with ginger, garlic and chives) were also delicious. For seafood lovers there is a seafood moilee, and a dhuae ki machchi (grilled monkfish and swordfish marinated in mustard, green chilli and lime leaf). The menu is changed every three months and expect to see new dishes from this young and enthusiastic chef.

Tiffin	1 De Montfort Street
££	Leicester
	LE1 7GE
	Tel: 0116 247 0420

Consistently voted among the best twenty restaurants in Leicester, this Indian restaurant offers traditional curries in a smart surrounding. The conservatory is an added attraction and booking is usually a must. Dishes are traditional Indian dishes like chicken bhuna, fish masala, shahi korma, rogan josh and Kashmir lamb. Tandoori platters include boti kebab, chicken tikka, seekh kebab, tandoori fish and paneer shashlik.

Veeraswamy	Mezzanine Floor, Victory House
£££	101 Regent Street
	London
	W1R 8RS
	Tel: 0207 734 1401

A location that can only be every restaurateur's dream, especially during the Christmas season, when you can look out at the lights over Regent Street. The new-look Veersawamy is smart and savvy, with bold colours and a few tasteful antiques that give it the special Indian ambience. Also the romance of being the oldest surviving Indian restaurant with plenty of history and old photographs to browse through. Namita Panjabi's menu is select and well defined for its regional flavours. Choose from starters like Achari chicken tikka, quail tandoori or mussels moilee. Main courses include Malvani prawn curry (from the Malabar coast), chicken salan (hot chicken pepper curry from Keala), sea bass pollichadu (sea bass marinaded in red Kerala-style masala, pan-fried in banana leaf), and lamb Travancore (lamb in spicy coconut sauce). Best to book windowside tables in advance during the festive season. Winner of the *Time Out* Best Indian Restaurant award in 1997.

Sister restaurant
Chutney Mary

Verandah	17 Dalry Road
£	Edinburgh
	EH11 2BQ
	Tel: 0131 337 5828

A popular Edinburgh restaurant that offers traditional Indian and Bangladeshi fare. Smart and clean decor with cane chairs and bamboo slats on the walls. Dishes from the tandoor including a variety of kebabs and fish tikkas and curries including rogan josh and chilli garlic chicken.

Zaika	1 Kensington High Street
£££	London
	W8 5NP
	Tel: 0207 795 6533

Vineet Bhatia's path-breaking Michelin-star restaurant has quickly become one of London's most fashionable restaurants. Understated decor with a few antique carvings and an occasional dash of colour. There are poppadoms too (mini-snack size), with a tasty selection of pickles, though this is as far from a curry house as you can get. Food is traditional Indian with a little twist.

The seafood platter starter – Samundari Zaika – was delicious with distinct flavours from each fish. Also recommended are the trio of scallops (onion and sesame crusted, spice crusted and coconut milk and kokum poached scallop with chilli mash). For the main course take your pick from tikhi machi (pan-fried marinated sea bass served on an upma sauce) or crab risotto with grilled seafood, or spicy Mangalorean chicken. There is also the traditional rogan josh and butter chicken.

Vineet Bhatia's chocomosas (or chocolate samosas) served with ice cream are being copied in India and I am not surprised. They are delicious!

CHEAP AND CHEERFUL

Some cheap and cheerful places (without compromising on the food). All priced below £15 per person.

Adil
148–50 Stoney Lane
Sparkbrook
Birmingham
B12 8AJ
Tel: 0121 449 0335

One of the oldest balti restaurants in the area serving traditional balti food including the family naan. Winner of the Curry Club Best Balti Restaurant in 1999. Every conceivable combination in a balti – meat/spinach/mushroom balti, tropical balti, rogan josh balti, dhansak balti and plenty more.

Club 182
182–4 Preston Road
Wembley
Middx
HA9 8PA
Tel: 0208 908 6040

Great atmosphere in this Indian-style pub/restaurant which has beautiful old black and white photographs of cricketers, maharajahs and Indian politicians from the freedom struggle. A giant television screen plays either Bollywood songs or cricket. Atmosphere gets heated when India is playing. Cosy and comfortable and with a good menu of fish pakoras, jeera chicken, shish kebabs and other standard curries.

Diwana Bhel Poori
121 Drummond Street
Euston
London
NW1 2HL
Tel: 0207 380 0730

Functional café-style restaurant, open all day for snacks and meals.

Dosas, bhelpuri, papri chaat, all under a fiver. Hard to spend more than a tenner for good veggie food.

Imran's
264–6 Ladypool Road
Sparkbrook
Birmingham
B12 8JU
Tel: 0121 449 1370

One of the oldest balti restaurants in Birmingham and recently refurbished with smart clean interiors. Seekh kebabs, chicken tikka and balti specialities like balti prawn, balti chicken and balti vegetables. In-house sweet shop means there is a good variety of freshly made desserts and sweets.

India Club
143 The Strand
London
WC1 1JA
Tel: 0207 836 0650

An institution in itself, this place was started in 1950 by Krishna Menon in close association with the India League, which had its meetings at the India Club on the first floor of the building. Very much an Indian coffee-house atmosphere, with framed photographs of Gandhi and Krishna Menon on the wall. Dosas for breakfast if you fancy, and standard lamb, chicken and prawn curries for meals. All very reasonably priced. Still popular with Indian organisations and Indian diplomats from across the road at India House.

Karachi
15–17 Neal Street
Bradford
BD5 0DX
Tel: 01274 732015

Almost a Bradford institution, this restaurant has continued in the same vein for nearly forty years. No fuss, no cutlery, and practical formica-top tables. Kebabs, a variety of karahi dishes and a steady supply of hot chapattis that keep appearing on your plate. Always buzzing.

The Grand Junction Arms

Bulbourne
Tring
Hertfordshire
HP23 5QE
Tel: 01442 890677

A few miles' drive outside London into leafy Hertfordshire takes you to this canalside pub that's famous in the area as the Curry Pub. Great in summers with a big garden and sizzling barbecues.

Variety of dishes from Goa, Kerala, Sri Lanka and even Indonesia. Curry nights are a favourite with the locals.

Lahore Kebab House

Umberton Street
London
E1 1PY
Tel: 0207 481 9737

Another kebab lover's dream place and an institution in itself. Here is where it is served East End style. No fuss, no decor, simple long brown tables on which everyone sits together. The flow of hot naans is amazing, and the food is wonderful: karahi chicken, lamb, quail. A true dhaba atmosphere and one with quite a few celebrity visitors. Imran Khan has been here and Kapil Dev and even Bollywood icon Amitabh Bachchan. Strictly cash here since they have no time for plastics. A friend who went there, and found they did not accept credit cards, was told not to worry but enjoy his meal first and then go get the cash later. 'Paisa to aata hi rahega' (the money will keep coming), said the owner, which goes to show you can't beat the dhabas for sheer warmth and hospitality.

Nawab
32 Manor Row
Bradford
BD1 4QE
Tel: 01274 720371

The full service from poppadoms to pickles. Famous for its kebabs which have been eaten by many a celebrity. Traditional curries on the menu.

Pele's Balti Pub
1059 Foleshill Road
Coventry
CB6 6ER
Tel: 02476 686394

Famous balti pub of the Midlands which wants to expand into a British chain. Pele's menu has authentic food from Punjab. Decor very much Indian while retaining essential pub atmosphere. Traditional favourites include balti chicken speciality, balti chicken tikka masala, and balti badhsahi zafrani. Meal deals with a pint and a balti for under a tenner. Hard to go wrong.

Royal Naim
417–19 Stratford Road
Sparkhill
Birmingham
B11 4JZ
Tel: 0121 766 7849

Another old balti house in Birmingham that has won many awards. Chicken pakora, kebabs and a variety of baltis. Mixed vegetable balti, chilli garlic chicken balti and tropical balti. Family naans.

Sagoo and Thakkar   (New Asian Tandoori Centre)
114 The Green
Southall
Middx
UB2 4BQ
Tel: 0208 574 2579

The ultimate Punjabi dhaba. Expect to see the community here in full force giving it the certificate of authenticity. Self-service at the counter for chicken curries, lamb curries, daals and vegetables. Fast turnover and huge portions. Authentic Punjabi dishes like makki ki roti and sarson ka saag, aloo parathas, gobi parathas, and methi parathas. Kitchen reveals a sea of Punjabi men and women chopping and cooking. Great community feeling and the food is always good, if a bit oily.

Sakonis   19 Ealing Road
Wembley
HA0 4BP
Tel: 0208 903 1058

Started as a small takeaway counter in the late eighties and now is a full-fledged restaurant on the buzzing Ealing Road (famous for its ethnic shops selling jewellery, saris and Indian groceries) with a branch in Harrow that is strategically situated next to a cinema hall that shows Bollywood films. Dosas, chaat, bhelpuri, batata vada, even Indian-style Chinese and Indian-style pizzas. Strictly vegetarian. Expect to queue, especially over weekends.

Branch
Sakonis   6–8 Dominion Parade
Station Road
Harrow
HA1 2TR
Tel: 0208 863 3399

Glossary

amchur	dried mango powder used as a souring agent
anardana	pomegranate seeds also used as a souring agent
appa/appam	South Indian rice cakes
barfi	Indian sweetmeat
bhaji	Indian savoury
bhelpuri	a spicy mix usually eaten as a snack
bhindi	green vegetable – also known as okra or lady's fingers
bindi	a decorative dot worn on the forehead by Indian women
chapatti	Indian flat bread, also known as roti
daal	pulses
dahi	yoghurt
dhania	coriander
do-piaza	any kind of meat dish where the amount of onions is double that of the meat
dosa	a savoury pancake made of fermented rice and daal, usually cooked in South India
dumpukht	food cooked in 'dum' – pressure – with a sealed lid
gajar ka halwa	a rich sweet dish made out of grated carrots
gathia	Indian savoury

255

gulab	rose
haleem	a rich dish made of minced meat and broken wheat or oats
halwai	a sweetmeat maker
jalebi	an Indian sweet
jeera	cumin
karahi	a broad and deep cooking vessel resembling a wok
moong	a kind of pulse or lentil
mutka kulfi	a frozen Indian dessert set in small earthen containers
naan	Indian bread that is baked in a tandoor
nimboopani	fresh lime water
papad	poppadom
peda	a dry Indian sweet
rajbhog	Indian sweet served in sugar syrup
tandoor	clay oven, used for cooking tikkas, bread etc.
tikka	chunks of meat (lamb, chicken or fish) which is marinated and then grilled/ barbecued or cooked in a tandoor
thali	a large plate with a complete three or four course Indian meal. Indian restaurants often serve a thali, which is a complete Indian meal comprising daal, vegetables, meat or fish, rice, chapatties and a dessert

Bibliography

Achaya, K.T., *Indian Food: a Historical Companion* (Oxford University Press, 1994)

Allen, Charles (ed), *Plain Tales from the Raj* (Deutsch, 1975)

Atkinson, Captain G.F., *Curry and Rice on Forty Plates* (1854: reprinted by Asian Education Services, 1999)

Beeton, Isabella, *Mrs. Beeton's Book of Household Management* (1861: abridged edition, Oxford Paperbacks, 2000)

Brennan, Jennifer, *Curries and Bugles – Memoir and Cookbook of the British Raj* (Periplus, 2000)

Burton, David, *The Raj at Table – a Culinary History of the British in India* (Faber and Faber, 1993)

Chapman, Pat (ed), *The 2001 Good Curry Guide* (Simon and Schuster, 2001)

——, *Taste of the Raj: a Celebration of Anglo-Indian Cookery* (Hodder and Stoughton, 1998)

Chievers, Norman, Surgeon General, HM Indian Army, 'A commentary on the diseases of India' (J. & A. Churchill, London, 1886; Karnataka State Archives, file no. 411/1898/medical/excise)

Erickson, Carolly, *Her Little Majesty: the Life of Queen Victoria* (Robson Books, 1999)

Fay, Eliza, *Original Letters from India (1779–1815)*, edited by E.M. Forster (Hogarth Press, 1925)

James, Lawrence, *Raj: the Making and Unmaking of British India* (Abacus, 1998)

MacMillan, Margaret, *Women of the Raj* (Thames and Hudson, 1988)

Max, B., 'This and that: the essential pharmacology of herbs and spices', *Trends in Pharmacological Sciences*, 13 (1992), 15–20

Moulik, Achala, *Earth Is But a Star* (UBS, 1997)

Pruthi, J.S., *Spices and Condiments* (National Book Trust, New Delhi, 1998)

Visram, Rozina, *Asians in Britain: 400 Years of History* (Pluto Press, 2003)

Wellcome Institute of the History of Medicine, London, Mrs Turnbull's recipe notes (handwritten), MS 5853

Wilson, A.N., *The Victorians* (Hutchinson, 2002)

'Wyvern', *Culinary Jottings from Madras* (Madras, Calcutta & Bombay, 1878)

Yule, Henry and Burnell, A.C., *Hobson Jobson: a Glossary of Colloquial Anglo-Indian Words and Phrases* (1886: reprinted by Wordsworth Editions, 1996)

OTHER SOURCES

Information about curry can be found in various magazines that are aimed at an Asian audience or at the curry house industry, such as:

Eastern Eye (which publishes an annual supplement listing 'Britain's Richest Asians')
Tandoori, London

There are also various websites that provide information about curry itself, a variety of recipes, guides to restaurants, and personal accounts of the immigration experience:

www.movinghere.org.uk
www.curryhouse.co.uk
www.currypages.com
www.redhotcurry.com
www.clickwalla.com